ENDORSEMENTS

"A book that inspires with the loving guidance to instruct, is of great use to any Seeker. If you have picked up this book, you are a Seeker. You have found a guide for your travels. When we have journeyed through the abysses of the deepest of life's traumas and triumphs, as Sharon has; when we have seen the importance of finding union between our body, mind, and spirit, then we make room for our soul. Sharon carries us through that journey, with compassion combined with structured exercises, love interfaced with self-instruction, kindness actioned by schedule. Let your brain awaken with the guidance of this book. Let your mind wonder how it can still explore uncharted territories. Let your soul witness the yog, or union, of all the components that are You."

Bhaswati Bhattacharya, M.D., MPH, HHC, holistic physician, author; founder of the Dinacharya Institute for Wise Medicine, New York, NY

"Sharon Lund's book will inspire those of us who feel we are innocent victims; and she gives hope that we can change our attitudes, let go of the past and have a purpose in life that is greater than ourselves."

Gerald G. Jampolsky, M.D.
co-author of *A Mini Course for Life*
author of *Love is Letting Go of Fear*

THE INTEGRATED BEING:

ৡ ৶

THE INTEGRATED BEING:

Techniques to Heal Your Mind-Body-Spirit

SHARON LUND

Mar. 25, 09

To Vanessa —
You are a bright
light filled with
love and compassion.
I'm honored to
call you my friend.
Love & Blessings.
Sharon

Sacred Life Publishers™
www.sacredlife.com
United States of America

ॐ   ॐ

THE INTEGRATED BEING:
Techniques to Heal Your Mind-Body-Spirit

Copyright © 2009, by Sharon Lund

THE INTEGRATED BEING: Techniques to Heal Your Mind-Body-Spirit may be purchased or ordered through booksellers or by contacting:

Sharon Lund at
www.sharonlund.com

ISBN: 0-9822331-0-8
ISBN: 978-0-9822331-0-8
Library of Congress Control Number: 2008910937

The information, ideas, and suggestions in this book are not intended as a substitute for professional advice. Before following any suggestions contained in this book, consult your physician or mental health professional. Neither the author nor the publisher shall be liable or responsible for any loss or damage allegedly arising as a consequence of your use or application of any information or suggestions in this book.

Cover and text design: Miko Radcliff
Cover photo: Jeaneen Lund

Sacred Life Publishers
www.sacredlife.com
Printed in the United States of America

✧✧

I Dedicate The Integrated Being To:

❖ *Jeaneen, my beautiful daughter whose love inspired me to continue to live.*

❖ *Hector, for his unconditional love and devotion which opened my heart to the pure essence of love.*

❖ *Linda Dutton-Steindler whose bright light illuminated my path to healing.*

❖ *The magnificent men and women around the world who assisted me to become who I am today.*

❖ *You, the reader taking this journey as student and teacher.*

❖ *The teachers and students world-wide who bring forth Light, Truth, and Wisdom.*

❖ *Everyone embracing and working toward the Truth.*

"Humankind has not woven the web of life.

We are but one thread within it.

Whatever we do to the web, we do to ourselves.

All things are bound together.

All things connect."

~ Chief Seattle

CONTENTS

CHAPTER 1 – THE MIND

꙰   ꙰

CHAPTER 2 – THE BODY

☙ ❧

CHAPTER 3 – THE SPIRIT

ॐ   ॐ

APPENDIX

INTRODUCTION

As infants we are born into this world pure, innocent, beautiful, and loving. Yet in a matter of weeks, months, years, or decades, we may be shattered from neglect, abuse, or judgment from others and ourselves.

I was born Sharon Marie Clark in Seattle, Washington, in late November 1949. I was blessed with my parents, Tom and Jean Clark. My mother died in 1999 after many years of suffering with emphysema. My father is healthy, strong, vibrant, and instrumental in my life. Both my parents have been loving, wonderful, kind, generous, supportive, encouraging, and amazing.

I am the second born of four children. Tommy, the oldest, was my hero and best friend. My younger brother, Raymond, was often sick with several illnesses, which kept us from being close. Both Tommy and Raymond died at the age of 23, five years apart. Tommy was killed instantly in a motorcycle accident and Raymond died from an overdose of heroin.

My sister Joyce is nine years younger than me. She lives outside of California, so we are not able to see each other often. However, every day we call. Her friendship is important in my life.

In 1983, I became infected with HIV by my second husband, Bill, who led a secret bisexual lifestyle. I have faced many other life challenges, including nine years of sexual abuse as a child. I responded in various ways, including dealing with anorexia, suicide attempts, destructive relationships, and near-death experiences.

We can learn from our experiences and become empowered, or we can become victims—real or imagined—helpless, powerless, and blaming others. In contrast, an empowered person takes responsibility for their part, makes the most of circumstances, finds new ways to grow from challenges, and experiences inner peace. It is up to each individual to decide how to handle obstacles. I chose to live and thrive, but I needed tools.

My road to healing and peace took time and patience. Through two decades of mind, body, and spiritual experiences, I learned to heal my past, mind, body, and heart. I now want to share what I have learned with you. Throughout *The Integrated Being: Techniques to Heal Your Mind-Body-Spirit*, I weave in my life experiences, challenges, and lessons. I open my heart to you as I was guided to do in one of my near-death experiences.

As you read, you may be drawn to processes, visualizations, meditations, and much more that can help you make conscious choices that allow your challenges and circumstances to empower you and help you embrace your authentic self.

By facing all of my challenges and releasing them, I have been able to see them as sacred, because they have healed me, brought me to self-discovery, to wholeness, and to living my life purpose.

In 1987, I was one of the first women infected with HIV to go public in Southern California. For the next 10 years I was an advocate, extremely active in the HIV/AIDS community, and instrumental in setting up new programs in the United States and Russia.

I was the first infected woman elected to serve on the Board of Directors for AIDS Project Los Angeles (APLA), AIDS Medicine and Miracle, the International AIDS Project, and the Los Angeles County Health Service HIV Planning Council. I was an active member of the Women's Caucus of the AIDS Regional Board, and the AIDS Task Force of Southern Utah. I am currently a member of the International Community of Women Living with HIV/AIDS (ICW), San Diego Council on Aging, and the San Diego Bereavement Consortium.

My journey has taken me throughout the United States and into Canada, Europe, Russia, and Japan where I taught classes and workshops, met wonderful people, and learned even more. I have appeared on *The Oprah Winfrey Show, 48 Hours, Eye on America*, and *CNN,* and been featured on the front page of the *Los Angeles Times*. Part of my life story was featured in the November 2007 issue of *O, The Oprah Magazine*.

Our life is a precious gift from Infinite Spirit. What we do with our life is up to each of us, and it is our gift back to God, humanity, and the Universe.

Love and Blessings,

Sharon Lund

Suggestions

As you read through *The Integrated Being: Techniques to Heal Your Mind-Body-Spirit,* be open to possibilities you may never have thought of or experienced before. There may be some sub-chapters that resonate more with you that you will want to incorporate into your life or learn more about. Other sections may not agree with you, which is fine.

Remember these points:

1. I am not a medical professional. I am a woman who has overcome many life-challenging obstacles and it is my desire to share my knowledge with you. It is important to consult your physician or mental health professional for expertise.

2. The human body is a complex organism with the innate ability to heal itself when given the proper tools. Some of the information and methods of healing I have used may not feel comfortable to you. Therefore, take what you are drawn to and leave the rest behind. What is important is that you find a path to wellness with which you feel comfortable. You may choose Western therapies, Alternative, or perhaps a combination of both—Integrative Medicine. Whatever methods of healing seem true to your soul, spirit, mind, and body are the ones that will work best for you.

3. Regardless of which treatments you choose, when approaching a holistic lifestyle you want to incorporate

methods to heal the mind, body, and spirit in order to bring yourself back into balance and wellness.

4. In *The Integrated Being* each chapter and sub-chapter builds up to the next one. However, it is not necessary to read the book from cover to cover. You may do a quick overview and find you are drawn to The Spirit Chapter first and then go back and read sections in the Mind and Body Chapters.

5. As you read through the chapters and sub-chapters, you can write your notes in the back of the Appendix, starting on page 337.

6. Every body is different, so what works for one person may not work for another. Get to know your body.

7. Each process, visualization, and affirmation is numbered or broken down into steps. It is important to pause between each number or step, so you can get the full impact of what is being said or taking place.

8. Although I have broken down *The Integrated Being* into three main chapters and categories The Mind, The Body, The Spirit, many topics could have been placed in all three chapters—as all are integrated.

9. I have chosen to connect the Mind-Body-Spirit instead of writing Mind, Body, and Spirit, because it is my desire that you see the connection between the three—and everything.

10. Every person has their own connection to what is true to their spirit, their soul, and their heart. Throughout *The Integrated Being* I use the words Infinite Spirit and God,

as they are two of the many words I call my Source of Life and the Creator of All. There are hundreds of words you can replace for the word God or Infinite Spirit. Please use whatever word resonates with you.

11. You hold the answers <u>within</u> you, and these tools can help you access your higher and inner wisdom.

THE MIND

The Mind

The mind is a powerful instrument which can create or destroy. We are the creators of our mind, yet from time to time we allow our mind to control us. We allow outside influences, experiences, or challenges to dictate who we are. Sometimes the voices we hear in our mind may not even be ours. Perhaps we hear our parents, teachers, clergy, a schoolmate, society, culture, or a spouse. Some voices might be louder than others. With the various voices in our mind, we may have forgotten who we are.

Our self-esteem and self-image play an important part in the mind. Self-esteem has two parts: a feeling of personal competence and a feeling of personal worth. Self-esteem is the sum of self-confidence and self-respect.

For the first 35 years of my life, I had low self-esteem. From the outside, I looked and acted as if I had it all together, but on the inside, I was dying. I was killing myself, beating myself up with words, thoughts, and actions.

Nine years of being raped as a child, never feeling like I fit in at school, and some destructive and abusive relationships ripped me apart. I believed I was worthless, powerless, and undeserving. I attempted to cover up my feelings by becoming a people-pleaser, caregiver, and rescuer.

Our deepest vision of ourselves influences our significant choices and decisions, and therefore shapes the life we create for ourselves. Throughout this chapter about the mind, I will share with you the various techniques and processes that helped me to

3

heal and become whole again. As my self-concept, self-worth, and self-respect changed, my victim destiny changed. In my mind I am a hero. I faced my demons and took charge of my mind and my life. I am proud of who I am. I realize I am the creator of my life and my reality.

Self-Esteem

Millions of boys, girls, men, and women have low self-esteem because of various reasons.

My low self-esteem started at a young age. Being raped ripped me apart. I lost confidence and respect for myself. I felt filthy, betrayed, helpless, and ashamed. I blamed myself and hated my body. Confusion, frustration, anger, resentment, fear, hatred, and depression silently filled the pores of my being. Nightmares of being molested by my grandfather haunted my waking hours as much as it did my restless sleeping nights.

Up until high school, students called me names like stupid, toothpick, and pancake. I believed everything I heard and accepted it as the truth. I was skinny and flat-chested. Being stupid was due to what is known now as "dyslexia." I repeatedly transposed my letters and numbers, which made it difficult for me in math and reading. D's were common on my report cards. It's not that I didn't try, I just couldn't comprehend what I read.

Perhaps you or a friend of yours was called names such as fatso, nerd, four eyes, buck teeth, grease ball, loser, retard, or klutz. Children believe what they hear and, like me, probably accept it as truth. With these words a child loses confidence and self-respect. They may feel so bad about themselves, they start to stay away from others. The anger and madness can boil up inside where they may have thoughts of doing harm to themselves, or another person.

Show children how much they are loved. Let them know they are perfect just the way they are and everyone is unique and blessed in their own way. Reinforce their assets. Let them know you are there for them and they can come to tell you anything—even secrets! Always leave the door of communication open to children. Who knows what they have experienced at their young age. Millions of boys and girls have been molested and there are far too many silent children.

Children do not want parents to know how bad things are. There were numerous times I faked illness to stay home from school, and sometimes, I actually ended up sick due to the stress from being teased. Children who are being ridiculed in school may not want you to talk to a teacher or the other parents, but it is important to let teachers know what is happening.

In my life I had three abusive relationships. One was with my grandfather, another with a boyfriend, and one was a marriage that led to my self-destructive behaviors. Killing myself seemed to be the only way to release my pain and suffering.

Some of my deepest and darkest hours were transformed through the teachings of Dr. Nathanial Branden, a well known psychotherapist. Between 1985 and 1990, I read every book he wrote, did the exercises and assignments in the books, attended his seminars, and applied what I learned from him. He made a profound difference in my life and well-being. I attribute much of the raising of my self-esteem to his remarkable words and work.

Dr. Branden has written a lot of insightful, and timeless books. *How to Raise Your Self–Esteem: The Proven Action–Oriented Approach to Greater Self-Respect and Self-Confidence* was the first book that resonated with me on the importance of self-esteem and how to obtain it. I truly believe every family would benefit from reading this book. I also found a lot of value in his book, *Six Pillars of Self-Esteem*, as well as several of his workbooks, including *To See What I See and Know What I Know: A Guide to Self-Discovery*. I came to realize without self-esteem it was extremely difficult to succeed, love myself, or feel whole. In *How to Raise Your Self-Esteem*, Dr. Branden states, "Of all judgments we pass in life, none is as important as the one we pass on ourselves."

In 1985, I started to work with my teacher and mentor, Linda Dutton-Steindler, on Dr. Branden's *"sentence stems."* At first they seemed easy, but then they started to reach my core issues. I discovered thoughts, behaviors, and actions that did not serve me. Many of my actions and beliefs came from other people, such as my parents, situations that happened to me, church, and society. Through the processes and sentence completions, I was able to discover what triggered some of my actions and behaviors. Before long, I started to take full responsibility for my life and well-being.

What are sentence completions or sentence stems? When a sentence has been started and without taking time to think, you complete the sentence at least 10 times. I have found when I reach the eighth, ninth, and tenth answer, something very important (like the core issue) is brought to my awareness.

Some of the sentence stems I have used from Dr. Branden's books are:

- ❖ "Ever since I was a little girl . . ."
- ❖ "Sometimes when I am afraid I . . ."
- ❖ "One thing I had to do to survive was . . ."
- ❖ "Sometimes when I hurt I . . ."
- ❖ "If I deny and disown my pain . . ."
- ❖ "Sometimes I wish people knew . . ."
- ❖ "I am becoming aware . . ."

❖ "If my life belongs to me . . ."
❖ "One of the thoughts I push out of my mind is . . ."

The one sentence stem that turned my life around was, "If I was responsible for my life . . ."

As I filled in the first seven answers to this stem, nothing major came up, but the eighth, ninth, and tenth sentence completions changed my life forever.

8. "If I took responsibility for my life. . . my mother would not feel loved."
9. "If I took responsibility for my life. . .my mom would not love me anymore."
10. "If I took responsibility for my life. . .my mom would die."

That was a "wake up" call. I had been so enmeshed with Mom I had lost sight of my own self. Somehow I came to believe my life, well-being, and happiness revolved around my mom. When I came to the realization of how I had prioritized her, I was able to step back and look upon her with love and respect, and know in my heart if I took responsibility for my life, my mom would not leave me or ever stop loving me. If it had not been for the use of this sentence completion, I may still be trapped in false beliefs that would hold me back from being who I am today.

What Dr. Branden's sentence stems allowed me to do was get in touch with my unexpressed emotions, work with the core issues, and release false beliefs. What I gained was self-confidence, self-respect, understanding, forgiveness, self-love, courage, empowerment, and the truth—I Am A Magnificent Being!

I will never forget what my grandfather did to me. However, in time I learned how to function as a whole being, and how to love myself unconditionally—all of which is included throughout *The Integrated Being*.

Another Way to Use Sentence Completions

I have also used the following method of sentence completions while incorporating affirmations. This is a powerful way to change thought patterns and beliefs.

❖ Take a piece of paper and divide it in half. On the left side write something you deserve, such as:

> I deserve happiness
> I deserve to be successful
> I deserve love

Work with one issue at a time. After you write down your statement on the left side of the paper, read it aloud and then write your response on the right side. You may find you repeat the answer a few times, and that is fine. What is important is that you write as fast as you can without thinking ahead.

Repeat this process until you come up with 10 positive statements in a row on the right side of your paper. If you discover you get as far as number 9 without a negative thought, but number 10 is negative, continue to work on the same sentence stem until you come up with 10 positive statements in a row. You may find you work with a statement for two or three days, or weeks, before coming up with 10 positive responses.

As an example:

> I deserve happiness   Who told you that?

I deserve happiness	You are crazy.
I deserve happiness	That is a lie.
I deserve happiness	Who are you kidding?

12 pages later

I deserve happiness	1. Yes you do.
I deserve happiness	2. That's for sure.
I deserve happiness	3. Yes you do.
I deserve happiness	4. I'm happy you finally feel that way.
I deserve happiness	5. Indeed you do!

Once you come up with 10 positive statements in a row, your belief begins to change and you can go on to another statement. This is a fun process as you listen to the voices in your head and conquer them.

I deserve to be successful	Who are you kidding?
I deserve to be successful	Not in this lifetime.
I deserve to be successful	Don't be foolish.
I deserve to be successful	No you don't.

20 pages later

I deserve to be successful	1. Yes you do.
I deserve to be successful	2. As successful as you desire.
I deserve to be successful	3. Absolutely.
I deserve to be successful	4. Indeed you do.
I deserve to be successful	5. That's right!

Begin to enjoy the process and embrace the positive voices in your mind. Today, this moment is the only time you have the power to change anything.

As your self-esteem increases, you and people around you may notice changes such as:

1. Your face looks more relaxed.
2. Your eyes look brighter.
3. You stand up straighter, and your shoulders are relaxed.
4. You speak with confidence and want to be heard.
5. When you talk to people you look into their eyes.

If you have struggled with low self-esteem, it is never too late to let go of the past and learn to embrace who you truly are. Self-esteem is at the core of everything. With self-esteem you will experience more confidence, inner peace, courage, success, and begin to express your true essence.

≈   ≈

Co-Dependency

Co-dependency went hand-in-hand with my low self-esteem. When I first heard about co-dependency from Linda, it was hard to believe she was talking about me. After all, I was out to please everyone. EXACTLY! Everyone, except myself.

Co-dependency is all actions, feelings, and thoughts from the perspective of the False Self rather than the True Self. There are numerous characteristics of a co-dependent, but I will use my old characteristics as an example:

1. I always put other people's needs and wants before mine.
2. I felt and assumed responsibility for other's feelings and behaviors.
3. I had difficulty expressing my feelings; it did not matter if I was happy, sad, angry, frustrated, or joyful. When I did express my feelings, I would minimize them.
4. It was extremely difficult for me to make decisions. I valued other people's opinions more than my own and needed to receive their approval.
5. I allowed other people's actions, feelings, and attitudes to determine how I responded or reacted.

Along with the co-dependent behaviors, I also had control issues which were carried out in the following ways:

1. I thought and felt most people were incapable of taking care of themselves, so I took on the job for them.
2. I agreed with others so they would like me.
3. I gave, and gave, and gave to those I cared about.

4. I had to feel needed in order to have a relationship with others.
5. I was the strong and calm person when others were in crisis.

I believed these actions were showing how unselfish I was because I dedicated my life to others and always put them first. The reality was I was enmeshed in co-dependency.

Until I gained self-esteem, I didn't know how to set boundaries. In fact, I didn't know what boundaries were. These are some of the major boundary issues I experienced:

1. I engaged in self-abuse—mental, physical, and spiritual.
2. I allowed other people to direct my life and well-being.
3. I believed others should be able to anticipate my needs and read my mind.
4. I allowed other people to define who I was.
5. I didn't recognize when someone else invaded my boundaries, mainly because I didn't have any.

Then I became a professional "Enabler" which was demonstrated by the following:

1. I encouraged countless people to be helpless.
2. I did all I could to avoid problems and keep peace and harmony in my environment.
3. I minimized destructive behavior such as, "This is a one-time thing—he will never abuse me again."
4. I took on the full responsibility for all the financial support, (rent, food, entertainment, and much more) even when my husband had a full time job.
5. I covered up consequences and pretended events didn't happen.

My list could go on and on. For years, I thrived on living a life of co-dependency, where I never set boundaries and everyone else ruled.

Linda had me focus on several affirmations to help me, while I started to gain self-esteem.

- ❖ I am willing to forgive.
- ❖ I am grateful for my life.
- ❖ I deserve to be loved by myself and others.
- ❖ I respect my own and others' boundaries.
- ❖ I am beautiful inside and out.

As you read about co-dependency and the issues that surround it, you may feel the way I used to, which was, "I am showing love by all I do." The reality is I wasn't showing love. I was selfish and didn't allow people to be themselves, live their lives, or allow myself to embrace my life. I didn't consider what was important to me, because I didn't matter. They did! Remember it is okay to say "no" to things you don't want to do. It isn't being selfish. It is you taking care of yourself.

I learned to stop caring about other people's thoughts and opinions. Those belonged to them—not me. It makes absolutely no difference what people think of me. I had to start thinking and acting on what was right for me. My only obligation was to be true to my Spirit.

There are two powerful books written by Melody Beattie entitled, *Codependent No More: How to Stop Controlling Others and Start Caring for Yourself,* and *Beyond Codependency: And Getting Better All the Time.* If you are caught up in co-dependency in any way these books can change your life.

My journey out of co-dependency led to my happiness and peace of mind. Love yourself first and everything falls into place.

Your Attitude

Attitude has a lot to do with healing. You can be a victim and blame others, or you can become empowered and take responsibility. You can be angry, rude, and annoying to others, or you can embrace your challenges and discover ways to overcome them. When problems arise, face the challenge, and find the good in everything.

People are fun to be around when they are happy and have a good attitude. People who don't have anything good to say are difficult to be around, unless you enjoy negativity.

With *dis-ease*[1] I knew within my core being that in order to heal, I had to have a good attitude. It didn't matter if I was sick in bed or in the hospital; I had to wake up each morning and thank Infinite Spirit I was alive.

Here are some insights about attitude:

❖ When I awaken in a bad mood, it is important to make a conscious choice to turn my bad mood around. Once I discover what caused my mood change, I look at the brighter side and read my gratitude journal.

---

[1] * *dis-ease* — In Louise L. Hay's book *The Power Is Within You*, "disease is spelled *dis-ease* and denotes anything that is not in harmony with you and your environment." Throughout *The Integrated Being* I have chosen to use the word *dis-ease* in this way.

❖ My attitude determines my energy level and affects my health. If my attitude is positive, then my energy level is high. If my attitude is negative, I feel down, sluggish, exhausted, and irritable.

❖ I realize my attitude doesn't depend on what others say or think about me or any given situation. My attitude depends on what I say and think about myself and the situation. I am the only person responsible for my attitude. The blame goes no further.

❖ My attitude is formed from my feelings, emotions, and will.

❖ My thoughts create whether I feel comfortable or uncomfortable. I can choose to feel how I want by looking at the benefit of each situation. I am the only person in control of my thoughts and attitude.

❖ The more I express gratitude, love, joy, happiness, and compassion, the more my attitude is uplifting and positive.

❖ I reflect upon my life in a positive way. No matter what challenges I face, each contains a gift of learning.

❖ There are millions of men, women, and children who have it worse than I do.

❖ I am in charge of my life. I can rethink any situation and make a new choice.

❖ Attitude is the light in my heart. How bright it shines depends on my attitude.

Wake up in the morning with a smile upon your face. Begin the day with a positive attitude regardless of your circumstances. Do whatever it takes to carry your positive attitude throughout the day and night.

I remember the time my daughter and I finished giving an HIV/AIDS presentation at a university in Los Angeles. When we walked to the parking lot we found a huge tree had fallen on top of our car and covered two other cars as well. We couldn't even see the cars. Jeaneen and I laughed so hard we had tears in our eyes. One of the other car owners had a different attitude. She yelled, screamed, cursed, and blamed everyone but Mother Nature. Her attitude was irritating. Jeaneen and I stayed calm, realized it was only a car, and life was more important than a material possession. My car could be replaced, but our lives are what Jeaneen and I embraced.

My greatest accomplishment concerning attitude was my refusal to become a victim when I became infected with HIV/AIDS. Instead, I embraced the *dis-ease* and made the most of my life. I never blamed my ex-husband, Bill. I found HIV/AIDS to be a blessing because I no longer took life for granted. I discovered my life purpose. I did all I could to educate myself in a holistic way to stay healthy. I discovered what and who was important in my heart and soul. Now I live each day to the fullest. Moreover, I embrace life one moment at a time because that is all we have. One moment at a time! So, make the most of it with a positive attitude. Remember, in our challenges lie opportunities to redefine how we respond to life, people, and the world.

You are responsible for your choices, actions, and happiness. What choices and actions do you choose? You have the power to change your choice at any moment!

❧   ☙

Your Thoughts and Beliefs Create Your Reality

To hear your thoughts and beliefs create your reality can be tough to embrace. At least it was for me, especially with all my challenges. Yet, once I understood the process of my thoughts, it became clear to me indeed, my thoughts and beliefs were creating my future and my reality.

Remember all we are is energy. Therefore, whatever energy or vibration we are putting out, we are attracting back to us—positive or negative. We create through our thoughts. We can deliberately set into motion that which we desire. As I began to recognize my negative patterns and beliefs, I stopped focusing on them and thought about what I really wanted. As I focused on detoxifying my mind of negative thoughts, positive thoughts appeared clearer and more often.

❖ The Law of Attraction and The Law of Creation are universal. It doesn't matter if you believe in them or not; they affect you, even if you don't embrace them. It is all about where you are vibrating in any moment, in the current moment of every day.

Wherever you place your focus, attention, or energy, and therefore vibrate, is what you will be attracting into your life experience because "that which is like unto itself is drawn" (Abraham-Hicks). This places responsibility for EVERYTHING IN YOUR LIFE on you and only you. No one else can "do" anything to you because you are the one who has attracted whatever it is in the first place. The other person was only brought into your experience by your own focus and attention to fulfill your belief. So if something undesirable happens to you, you must step back and ponder, where have I been focusing my attention? How did I bring this event into my life? Where do my beliefs lie? Of course, if your life is going well, you can ask the same questions.

The next question is, "What would I rather have happen?" Turn your focus and attention to this question and really define what you want. Then place yourself there with all the smells, colors, sounds, tastes, and circumstances. This will begin to "pre-pave" events for the future. The more often you can place yourself in these very positive scenarios, the more you will move your vibration to a higher frequency which will begin to attract those more positive elements. It is all the same to "the Universe," good or bad. There is no judgment. It is up to you and your own thought process what you will experience in your life.

We are connected to everything. We are a vibrating mass of energy, intimately connected to this vast stream of energy that makes up the universe. I believe this is what Infinite Spirit is, and I am a tiny particle or wave of it. As I vibrate in more positive ways, I add to the "God energy," and I feel harmony with it all. When I resist change, or dwell on the negative, I move away from Infinite Spirit and consequently feel bad. This is how you can always tell just where you are vibrating—by whether you feel good or bad. It is that simple (or complicated). It takes being aware as much as possible of how you feel in any moment.

Remember, seek joy, first and foremost.

Some of my beliefs used to be:

- ❖ I am fat.
- ❖ I am stupid.
- ❖ I am skinny.
- ❖ I cannot trust men.
- ❖ To earn money I have to struggle.

My belief "I cannot trust men" went something like this: Men are untrustworthy. Men are abusive. Men are only out to please themselves. Men are stronger than me. I cannot stand up for myself. It is not wise to trust men.

From my thoughts about men, I ended up attracting a couple of relationships that proved my beliefs to be right. Even though I formed my beliefs about men at an early age from being raped, my thoughts were still so strong, and my vibration attracted what I focused on, whether conscious or not.

Beliefs can come from outside of us. We start to absorb other people's beliefs at an early age and then we grow up believing them.

In 1985, Linda first introduced me to the power of my thoughts and how they create my reality. I consciously started to watch my thoughts, and they quickly changed. Then I decided to practice creating with my thoughts and bringing about a new reality.

My daughter and I wanted to move into a house in Hollywood, California so she would be closer to her acting and modeling jobs. I didn't have money in the bank because of hospital bills. I had been out of the hospital with anorexia a short time, and I didn't have good credit, let alone a job. Linda told me miracles can happen through prayer, visualization, and positive thoughts. So every day I visualized exactly what Jeaneen and I wanted, with excitement, joy, and expectancy. I saw Jeaneen and myself living in the house we desired.

I *never* allowed FEAR (False Evidence Appearing Real) to enter my visualization or my thoughts (fear of not having the money, fear of not being able to get the house we wanted, fear of the landlord not accepting us). Instead, I stayed focused day and night on what Jeaneen and I desired.

I wrote every detail about our new home, thought about it throughout the day, and read what I wrote in the morning and before I went to bed. I wanted to live close to a grade school for Jeaneen. I wanted to live in a safe neighborhood with girls Jeaneen's age. We wanted a two-bedroom house with a study, laundry room with appliances, a nice large bathroom, a large kitchen with plenty of cupboards and a lot of counter space, a front room with a fireplace, a large dining room (big enough for my table and chairs, china hutch, and chest), a lot of windows to let in light, carpeted throughout, an extra room for storage, a large fenced-in backyard for a dog, a patio, nice friendly neighbors, private driveway, a nice clean-looking house inside and outside, affordable price, and a nice, dependable, friendly landlord.

When I wrote about what we wanted, I added a lot of feelings, such as excitement and joy of hearing the laughter of children playing, birds singing in the trees, the smell of fresh baked cookies, pizza, and chicken filtering throughout the house, and the feel of deep, soft carpet on our bare feet. I went through every room and added feelings and emotions to them. Then Jeaneen and I read it every morning and before we went to bed. I also kept the vibration of what we wanted in my mind throughout the day.

Then we drove around areas of Hollywood until we were led to Larchmont Village. I located the grade school, and for two weeks I drove around an area of six blocks in each direction from the school. Within the month, through my prayers, visualization, and the power of my thoughts, we found a beautiful home a block away from the school with everything Jeaneen and I wanted. The fantastic confirmation was I was able to rent the house with less than $125 in my bank account, with no down payment, and no security deposit. I met with the landlord; he loved me and Jeaneen and could tell we would be reliable tenants. He allowed us to move in the first month for free and pay the rent back within six months. We lived in our dream home for nine years.

This was one of many beautiful experiences that came through the power of my thoughts and intentions. I continue to draw events and people into my life whom I desire. Never doubt the power of your thoughts and words, especially when you put emotions with them. Create your reality the way you want your life to be.

Dr. Wayne Dyer states, "Learn to live the life you have imagined."

Buddha teaches, "All that we are is the result of what we have thought. If a man speaks or acts with an evil thought, pain follows him. If a man speaks or acts with a pure thought, happiness follows him, like a shadow that never leaves him."

There are several movies and books that have made a profound difference in the way a lot of people view their thoughts:

❖ *What the Bleep Do We Know!?* brought a new awareness of the power of our creation through our thoughts. On a scientific level it shows proof our thoughts create our reality.

❖ *The Secret* captured the attention of millions of people around the world and brought about the understanding of manifestation and how our thoughts create our reality.

❖ In *The Moses Code,* some of the best-known spiritual teachers in the world join James F. Twyman and offer tools that show us how we can apply the Moses Code to our lives. For years I have used the saying, "I Am That I Am." However, I learned in *The Moses Code* that by adding a comma it changes everything: "I Am That, I Am." This states we are everything. I Am That, I Am.

❖ The movie *Dalai Lama Renaissance* is a documentary narrated by Harrison Ford. Forty of the world's most innovative thinkers met with the Dalai Lama to solve many of the world's problems. At the end of the movie, the message I received was the presence of compassion heals and furthers our evolutionary stages as it brings together the opposites.

❖ Gregg Braden states in his video *Walking Between the Worlds,* "When you are holding emotion in your body you are holding it in the liquid crystal of your body. . . The higher the vibration/frequency, the more complex and more waves there are per unit, and the lower the vibration, the fewer waves per unit."

Later he goes on to say, "Thought, feeling, and emotion can shift body chemistry. That may be the single most powerful and empowering tool that you have available to you in response to life; the ability to shift your body chemistry by choice, simply through knowing your emotions and what they mean to you."

* One of my favorite books of all time is *Way of the Peaceful Warrior: A Book That Changes Lives* by Dan Millman. It is a true story of his life, which was made into a powerful movie titled *Peaceful Warrior*.

* Neale Donald Walsch has made a profound impact with his series of books that began with *Conversations with God: An Uncommon Dialogue*. There is also a movie made about his life story titled *Conversations with God*.

* Louise L. Hay's movie, *You Can Heal Your Life,* covers topics she has been writing and presenting since the mid-1980s. She also weaves in her personal life experiences and how she applied the concepts in her life.

  Louise's book *You Can Heal Your Life* is a timeless classic. She was a pioneer in teaching people their thoughts create their reality.

* There is the beautiful book entitled, *The Hidden Messages in Water* written by Dr. Masaru Emoto. It proposes an eye-opening theory that shows how water is deeply connected to individual and collective consciousness. By using high-speed photography, Dr. Emoto discovered crystals formed in frozen water reveal changes when specific, concentrated thoughts are directed toward it. If you haven't seen his book, it is truly amazing and brings an awareness of the power of our words. Positive or uplifting messages such as *love* and *thank you* have a magnificent, complex, and colorful snowflake pattern. Negative words such as *hate* and *war* create patterns that are dull, incomplete, and distorted.

  What patterns are you holding in your body? What are you creating?

A lot of bookstores now carry packets of positive words, such as *love, gratitude, happiness, joy, excitement,* and *compassion* which you can stick on a water glass or bottle. You can also make your own just by using a piece of paper and writing the word down and taping it onto your glass of water or bottle. Or, you can use a Sharpie pen and write the word directly on the bottle. The vibration of the word will change your water, especially when you repeat the word aloud.

Dr. Emoto's research is shared with scientists from all over the world in the DVD *Water – The Great Mystery.*

❖ British Director and Producer, Martin Dunkerton, traveled the world to test Napoleon Hill's classic book *Think and Grow Rich,* which sold over 100 million copies. What is the key to unlocking the life you really want, finding the person you want to be with, and creating the wealth, happiness, and joy you seek? Martin set out to see if the 13 Mastermind Principles including desire, faith, imagination, power of the Mastermind, the mystery of sex transmutation, the sub-conscious mind, the brain, and the 6th sense Napoleon Hill writes about are true. He interviewed well-known people around the world, including Mark Victor Hansen, co-creator of *Chicken Soup for the Soul* and *The One Minute Millionaire* and Rev. Michael Beckwith. In Martin's powerful, and informative documentary, he shares the secret to wealth and unlocking prosperity and seeing money in a different way. His documentary will be released summer/fall 2009. I was inspired as I watched a sneak preview of Martin's documentary while he was in San Diego. (The working title is *Think and Grow Rich).* For more information call 800-711-5903, Infinite Possibilities Productions.

❖ In Gregg Braden's book, *Spontaneous Healing of Beliefs: Shattering the Paradigm of False Limits,* he shows scientific proof everything is connected through a field of energy. Gregg states the importance of creating from our hearts instead of our minds. He mentions when we create from our hearts, energy is so much "purer" because it comes from Inner Being. When we create from our minds, we can mix up a lot of other beliefs and the results are far less rewarding. Gregg also shows how to heal false beliefs that may have limited you in the past.

In the May 2008 issue of *The Light Connection*, Gregg Braden said, "Everyone is born with the nonverbal language of the heart that communicates with our bodies and our world. If we can hone that language in just the right way, we can affect what seems like miraculous healings in ourselves and in the world. It's really all based on, 'feeling,' which we have discounted in the West."

Gregg goes on. "Our heart's magnetic field is as much as 5,000 times stronger than that of the brain. So when we create a feeling in our hearts, we are literally creating a pattern of energy that's stronger than any thought in our minds."

❖ Norman Cousins, author of *Anatomy of an Illness,* was diagnosed with Ankylosing Spondylitis. The doctors, one of whom was a close friend of Cousins, speculated his chance of survival was approximately 1 in 500. Cousins checked out of the hospital and went to a hotel where he watched funny films, including numerous Candid Camera tapes and the Marx Brothers movies. Cousins cured himself through laughter.

❖ Esther and Jerry Hicks present the teaching of the non-physical entities collectively known as Abraham. Wisdom from Abraham has been channeled to Esther and can be found in books such as *The Law of Attraction: The Basics of the Teachings of Abraham,* and *The Amazing Power of Deliberate Intent.*

The Abraham-Hicks center and library in San Antonio, Texas is filled with CDs on subjects such as self-esteem, finances, relationships, health, and career, so you could choose almost any subject and find a CD that is devoted to it.

"It's not who you are that holds you back, it's who you think you're not." ~ Anonymous

Each morning when you wake up, take some time and decide how you want your day, week, and life to be. Set your intent. When you go to bed look back and see how you did.

How could you change your perspective today to improve the quality of your life? Create your heart's desire. From the center of your heart, live in love and watch the world around you change.

Affirmations

The power in your words and thoughts creates reality. Consistent thinking patterns create experiences. As you change these patterns, you can change your experiences.

Affirmations are strong, positive statements verifying something already exists. They can be general or very specific.

Think about the conversations and beliefs inside your head. In your mind, do you hear these statements?

- ❖ I am fat.
- ❖ I am ugly.
- ❖ I am worthless.
- ❖ I am a disgrace to the family.
- ❖ I am stupid.
- ❖ I cannot do anything right.
- ❖ I will never amount to anything.

Negative thoughts and other people's beliefs controlled my life until Linda showed me how to use affirmations to diminish the negative voices. I wrote down two or three affirmations (no more at first) and then used small colored dots to represent each affirmation. I stuck the colored dots on different items such as the refrigerator, mirrors, telephones, doors, cupboards, and my hair brush. Every time I saw a colored dot, I would repeat the affirmation associated with it.

Here are a few examples:

- ❖ A yellow dot = It is safe to be me.
- ❖ A red dot = I love and approve of myself.
- ❖ A green dot = I lovingly forgive and release the past.

I also found it helpful to place dots around the area where I worked. When people asked me what the dots were for, I said, "They are just a reminder to me," and then they never asked anything more.

In 1985, Linda gave me a copy of Louise L. Hay's book, *You Can Heal Your Life.* It lists health problems, possible causes of illness, and affirmations. I gained insight and valuable information on health issues such as AIDS, anorexia, fatigue, lung problems, sore throats, and much more. I discovered the possible cause of a specific condition and picked an affirmation that resonated with me. To this day, I still use Louise's book and recommend it to everyone.

I used affirmations to help myself get out of a self-destructive mode. Within a month I began to notice a difference. Negative voices were not as loud, and when they crept in I was conscious of them and immediately stated an affirmation. The mind is powerful, and when it hears repetition of a positive phrase or affirmation, in time the positive behavior will manifest. Once I understood the power of my thoughts and the use of affirmations, I was able to reclaim my Spirit and my life.

It is important to write, say, sing, or chant your heartfelt affirmations in the present tense, as if it is happening already. "I am now in an amazing, wonderful, loving, supportive relationship." When you start an affirmation using the words "I AM" this brings about more power. "I am whole and complete within myself." Below are some affirmations I have collected and used throughout the years:

- ❖ I am honoring myself.
- ❖ I am open to abundance.
- ❖ I am debt free in a happy way.
- ❖ I am healthy in mind, body, and spirit.
- ❖ I am attracting harmonious relationships.
- ❖ I am an expression of the Divine.
- ❖ I am grateful for my life.
- ❖ I am allowing good to flow to me.
- ❖ I am living in the perfect home and environment.
- ❖ I am consciously and consistently experiencing inner peace.
- ❖ I am communicating with others in a way that reflects my inner self.
- ❖ I am easily finding myself loving, and accepting my partner for who he is.
- ❖ I am consciously and consistently experiencing love in all of my relationships.

As I write my affirmations, I often include words such as *consciously, consistently, flow,* and *easily.* Create and choose affirmations that feel right for you. Begin with short concise ones. Be creative as you make up your affirmations and then decorate your environment with colorful dots.

You may choose to record your affirmations and listen to them in the house, while you are driving, or before you go to sleep. If you decide to record your affirmations, you can use the "I am," or use your name and say them in the first, second, and third person. For example, say, "I, Sharon, deeply love and appreciate life," "Sharon, you are deeply loving and appreciating life," and "Sharon is deeply and lovingly appreciating life."

Enjoy the use of your words in a powerful way.

Incantations

A while back, I attended a four-day seminar led by Anthony Robbins, which was vigorous and insightful.

One of the techniques we used at different times throughout the seminar was incantations. This is a ritual of reciting words or special phrases, usually rhyming, in order to produce a magical effect. Incantations are like affirmations, but they are done with movement and the power of voice. Say the incantations with the emotions you want to attract.

For example, say "love" in a loving way. Say "strength" with power and strength. You can use the power of incantations to summon any quality or energy you want or need.

I have used incantations when I work out at the gym. "I am losing weight and feeling great." I stress the first "I" and repeat the sentence five times with the "**I**" sounding stronger than the other words. Then I move to "**am**" and punctuate it with movement, energy, and strength. For each word, I repeat the sentence five times, and then go on to the next word to accent. Another phrase I use is, "I am losing flab and feeling fab."

It is also fun to use incantations when you take brisk walks. "I am releasing stress with each step."

❧   ☙

Acknowledge Who You Are

Throughout my life, from time to time, I dwelled on what I call the negative aspects of me. When I began to understand my thoughts, I started to focus on my positive aspects.

I remember years ago I was introduced to a couple of exercises that opened my eyes to the beauty and truth of who I am. I would like to share these exercises with you.

- ❖ List on a sheet of paper all the qualities you like about the men, women, and children you admire and respect. I wrote qualities such as outgoing, honest, trustworthy, fun, educated, happy, peaceful, respected, loving life, and serving humanity. It was easy for me to see and write the remarkable qualities of other people I admired.

  Then I was asked to write all the wonderful qualities about ME! That was difficult. I couldn't think of very many. I wrote I was a good mother, kind, honest, and spiritual.

  I was then told to look at both lists side by side (the one about the other people and the one I made about myself.) I noticed a huge difference between the two lists. Then I realized I had at least 98% of the same qualities of those I admired! The only difference was I recognized it in them and not within myself.

How often do you compare yourself to others? When it comes to positive qualities about another person, realize the person is a mirror of who you are; otherwise, you wouldn't have noticed their magnificent qualities. This is true of the negative as well. What a teaching tool! We often get annoyed with others who display traits we deny or dislike in ourselves.

❖ Another exercise I recommend is similar, yet a little harder to do. On a piece of paper, write the numbers from 1 - 100. Without thinking, write as fast as you can the fabulous adjectives that describe you: who you are, what you do, the roles you play, and what you have going for yourself. Write down as many wonderful and amazing adjectives as you can without stopping, such as:

   1. Loyal
   2. Talented
   3. Trustworthy
   4. Friendly
   5. Generous
   6. Honest
   7. Spiritual
   8. Etc.... to 100

If you get stuck, ask your friends and loved ones to tell you some adjectives that describe you.

Once you have written your 100 adjectives, read them aloud and notice how you feel. Realize this is truly YOU! Whenever you get down or discouraged, read over your list of fabulous qualities, and embrace yourself.

I want to encourage you to take time to reflect on all that you are, all that you do, and all that dwells within your heart. You are a Magnificent Being!

Visualization

Visualization is something we do throughout the day and evening. You may be at work and look out the window and imagine you are at the beach basking in the warm sun, or perhaps on a golf course shooting par.

You can use Creative or Deliberate Visualization to manifest what you truly desire, such as a loving relationship, optimum health, prosperity, a home, and inner peace. The clearer and stronger your intention, the more quickly and easily your desire will manifest. When I do visualizations, I ask for what I desire, and then I add, "This or something better for my highest good." Sometimes, what we desire is not for our highest good, so tap into your Divine wisdom.

You can also use visualization to get in touch with your Guardian Angels and Spirit Guides. This process has been outlined in The Spirit Chapter, sub-chapter "Angels, Archangels and Spirit Guides."

Shakti Gawain has an informative book, *Creative Visualization: Use the Power of Your Imagination to Create What You Want In Your Life*, which covers topics such as "Basics of Creative Visualization," "Using Creative Visualization," "Meditations and Affirmations," "Special Techniques and Living Creatively." This book has been around for decades and will continue to be instrumental in people's lives for decades to come.

One of the easiest ways to get started in Creative or Deliberate Visualization is to find a comfortable place where you can relax and let go of any outside noises or influences. Take a couple of slow deep breaths; inhale through your nose and exhale through your mouth. Get in touch with what your heart desires. Hold your positive focus on that which you desire. Believe you truly can achieve it, and then be open to receiving it. As you visualize, use all the emotions and senses you can bring into your visualization—smell, taste, hearing, textures, shapes, colors, images, and more.

In visualizations some people can hear, some people can see, and others can feel or sense things. There are also some men and women who do all of the above. It doesn't matter what category you fit into. The exercise below will give you an idea if you use visual, auditory, or sensory perception.

1. Find a place where you won't be interrupted and you can sit or lie down in a comfortable position.

2. Gently close your eyes and let go of any outside noises, and relax. Pause.

3. Take a few slow deep breaths, in through your nose and out through your mouth.

4. Imagine you are walking barefoot on a beautiful, white sandy beach. Pause.

5. The sun is out and it is the perfect temperature for you. Pause.

6. Can you feel a warm breeze upon your face? Pause.

7. Continue to walk down the beach and feel the warm sand on your bare feet. Pause.

8. Now as you look into the distance, perhaps you can see children building a sand castle. Pause.

9. Can you hear the children giggle? Pause.

10. Continue to walk down the beach and see if you can hear the waves crash on the shoreline. Pause.

11. As you look out toward the ocean, perhaps you can see surfers enjoying their rides on the waves. Pause.

12. As you stand by the shoreline, imagine you smell the misty salt water and taste it on your lips. Pause.

13. Now slowly move your body and take a deep breath. When you feel comfortable open your eyes.

You are auditory if you could hear the waves crashing and the children giggle.

You are visual if you could see the white sand beach, the children building a sand castle, and the surfers.

You use the sense of feeling if you could feel the warm breeze on your face and the warm sand on your bare feet.

In this brief visualization, perhaps you were able to hear, see, or feel, or a combination. Whatever you received or did not receive is perfect. If nothing came to you, you will probably discover some of the processes will work better for you through writing, which will be discussed later.

It is powerful to use Creative or Deliberate Visualization just after waking up and just prior to going to sleep.

When I was sick with HIV/AIDS, I visualized a Pac-Man going through my body and blood stream eating up the virus. Or I would see brilliant bright light dissolving the virus. You can make up your own visualizations that feel comfortable to you.

Though it may seem contradictory, I have also come to know and love my virus. I would talk to it and ask it why it wanted to be so strong and take over my body. What lessons could I learn from what I was experiencing? What did the virus need in order for me to be healed? More of this is described in The Body Chapter, sub-chapter "Body Dialogue."

You Are Not Alone

Sometimes you may find it difficult to seek support. However, as I mention in The Spirit Chapter, sub-chapter "Make Your Needs Known," it is important to have support and realize you are not alone.

When I was growing up, I felt if I asked for support, the person would want something from me in return. That scared me because it brought up my sexual abuse. My support during the nine years of being raped by my grandfather was my baby doll named Susie, God, and my Angel of Love.

Now that I have healed my past, I feel comfortable asking for support—emotional, mental, physical, or spiritual. I have a lot of global friends; some of my friends I can talk to about many topics, and with others I choose to only share certain information. Not only does support come from friends, but it also comes from loving and supportive family and extended family.

When I was in high school, I had a favorite teacher, Sister Helena. She became my strength and support during my school days. My therapist has been a valuable wealth of support and stability in times of need. When I was involved with a congregation, I felt close to the minister and would open my heart and thoughts to her. My greatest support outside my family is my relationship with God/Infinite Spirit and my Spirit Guides and Angels. I never feel alone or unsupported, because I can always turn to prayer and meditation to feel a sense of inner peace and receive Divine Guidance.

Being infected with HIV in the mid-1980s was difficult. I was one of the first infected women with HIV/AIDS to attend Louise L. Hay's Hay Ride Support Group in Los Angeles. Louise was incredible, and she is as beautiful on the outside and she is on the inside. Louise and the gay men embraced me and showed me compassion, love, and understanding. I felt so close to these men that many of them became my closest friends. It made it that much more devastating when they died from AIDS complications. Even though I felt a deep connection to Louise and the men at The Hay Ride, a lot of women's needs and issues were not addressed.

In 1990, I started a Women's HIV/AIDS Support Group at a wonderful old Hollywood house that was a drop-in center for Northern Lights Alternatives, co-founded by my incredible friend, Sally Fisher, along with Victor Phillips and Chuck Biaer. This special center offered support, counseling, the AIDS Mastery Workshops, and social gatherings. Its members brought politics and spirituality together in the context of the epidemic. During this time there were only a few women who attended the Women's HIV/AIDS Support Group. However, we felt blessed to find one another and became special friends. When Northern Lights Alternatives had to close the house, it was a great loss.

Then I started a support group for Women Faced with Life Challenging Illnesses at Marianne Williamson's LA Center for Living. You could feel and sense the peacefulness Marianne created. As more women came together, we felt unified, empowered, resourceful, supported, uplifted, nurtured, and loved. After a while, it was time for me to let another woman step up and lead our support group.

It doesn't matter where you find support as long as the person is there for you in a positive, loving, and supportive way. You may turn to numerous people for different kinds of support. Know when you seek support, there is always someone special who cares about you and your needs, someone who encourages and inspires you, someone who believes in you, someone who will listen to you. Turn to those who can support you in all areas of your life. Do not ever feel alone!

If you discover your needs are not being met, perhaps it is time for you to get a group of people together to create that which you desire. Step out in faith and trust!

∂∞ ∞∂

Sub-personalities/Archetypes

Sub-personalities are within each of us. Sometimes people refer to sub-personalities as archetypes, such as the reformer, the helper, the achiever, the individualist, the investigator, the protector, the loyalist, the enthusiast, the challenger, and the peacemaker. Discovering which ones run your life can be enlightening. When you consciously become aware of your sub-personalities, you are able to step outside of them and just observe. As you observe your sub-personalities and their behaviors, your choices and lessons can empower you.

Throughout my years of working with my sub-personalities, the ones that show up the most are the protector, rescuer, and caregiver.

There are various ways to communicate with your main sub-personalities.

❖ Visualization. Gently close your eyes. Ask to set aside your ego, fears, and concerns to hear and see the truth for your highest good, in love and light. Begin by taking a few slow deep breaths to relax your body, emotions, and mind. Breathe slowly in through your nose, and as you exhale, let out a sound. Allow each breath to become deeper as you let go. Breathe in peace and let go of tension. Empty yourself. Once again breathe in peace and stillness. Allow yourself to feel safe.

Now imagine, sense, visualize, or see yourself walking down four stairs. With each step down, feel safe. At the bottom of the stairway is a door, and as you open the door, notice a large conference table in the middle of the room. You may be able to see, visualize, or imagine a man, a woman, an animal, an object, or yourself in disguise sitting in each chair. Don't be surprised if a sub-personality appears as a shape or object.

As they are seated, introduce yourself out loud to all the beings in the room. Allow them to tell you who they are. It might surprise you. One may say, "I am your hero," or another might say, "I am your advocate," "I am your rescuer," "I am your saboteur," "I am the eagle," or "I am a crystal." Whatever you sense, see, or hear, thank them for coming.

You may want to write their names. Now you know them individually, so ask each one the following:

1. What do you need from me?
2. What are your qualities?
3. In what situations do you flourish?
4. What are your weaknesses?
5. What are your strengths?
6. What situations do you feel least comfortable in?
7. What do you want out of life?
8. What do I need from you?
9. What are you here to teach me?
10. How long have you been part of my life?
11. Then ask: is there anything else you want to tell me at this time?
12. If you have any questions you want to ask them, feel free to do so.

Thank your sub-personalities for talking to you.

After you have listened to your sub-personalities, regardless if they appear to be persons, objects, or animals, you will learn how to work with your dark (negative) and light (positive) aspects.

If you find it difficult to do this visualization in the conference room, then communicate with your sub-personalities using the chair-to-chair process that is outlined in this chapter, sub-chapter "Voice Dialogue."

Drawing is another way to discover your sub-personalities. Look over the list of some of the names of sub-personalities, and then draw what comes to mind when you think of one. Write out your impressions of this sub-personality.

Once you have discovered the main sub-personalities in your life write their names and see how they complement and help each other. After you pair them up, let them have a dialogue with each other so you can learn and discover what they are doing in your life.

From the Native American Indian traditions I have learned to work with my totem animals such as the bear, deer, eagle, beaver, elk, butterfly, and others. As I grow and change, I draw in new animal medicine to me.

Carl Jung includes the following as Archetypes: The Shadow, The Syzygy (Divine Couple), The Child, and the Self.

Caroline Myss and Peter Occhiogrosso state in *Sacred Contracts: The Journey,* "Of the 12 archetypes in our personal support team, we all share 4: The Child, Victim, Prostitute, and Saboteur. Each of these is deeply involved in our most pressing challenges related to survival."

Dharma Singh Khalsa, MD states in *The End Of Karma,* "We all have many sides of our personalities, from the shadow to the light. While it may be somewhat fashionable, philosophically interesting, or psychologically important to know all sides of yourself, I'm not one to say, 'Embrace your dark side. Embrace your shadow.' In contrast, I say, 'Manifest your light until your shadow disappears.' That's dharma."

As a lifetime member, I attend various dynamic, insightful, playful, and creative workshops with a brilliant man by the name of Clinton Swaine, the founder of Frontier Trainings, The World Leader in Experiential Games Technology. In one of his workshops, we dress up in costumes that fit 12 archetypes and then act out different situations or stories in our lives. I am amazed at how powerfully and accurately the characters come to life when I am dressed as their personality. I have discovered parts of me I never knew existed. Now that I am aware of them, I can call any archetype's personality I choose, which allows me to flow easily through life.

Begin to know your sub-personalities or archetypes, and as you have fun with them, let your light shine brighter.

Sandplay

One of my therapists, Gita Morena, specializes in Sandplay, which is a Jungian type of therapy using symbolic language. I always look forward to our sessions. I am like a little girl anxiously waiting to play in the sand and see what I create. Whatever issue or challenge I am faced with, we first talk about it, and then I walk around her room where she has thousands of miniature figurines. Without thinking, I find myself drawn to various figures and I place them in the sand box. She notes the order and position of each item. Sometimes I may be drawn to only a few things, other times I may have 20 or more figurines in the sand. After I feel complete, we look over the sand box and suddenly a story unfolds before my eyes. Through free, creative play my unconscious is made visible in a three-dimensional form and a pictorial world.

Playing the Game!

Dr. Phil McGraw talks about the payoff and cost of things we do. What is the hidden agenda behind the things you say and do? What are your actions and words really saying? What is the truth behind them?

During my dark days of negative patterns, Dr. Phil was unknown to me. I learned about "Playing the Game" from my therapist and the book, *A New Day in Healing* by Valerie Seeman Moreton.

To discover patterns in your life, answer the following questions. You may choose to write the questions first so you can examine your answers.

1. What is the biggest complaint about your life? What is the pattern that keeps repeating itself and leaving you frustrated?

2. What are the negative decisions you have made about yourself? (This is the "perpetuation" i.e. I am not..., I can't....)

3. What is your payoff? In what way do you get to be right about your inability to be who you want to be? What discomfort do you try to protect yourself from (i.e. I avoid..., I get to....)

4. What is this costing you? How is your life being affected by this? (i.e. my health..., my happiness....)

5. Is it worth it? (Yes or No)

6. How do you compensate for your perpetuation, for failing at what you really want to be? (Because of not…, I must do … to compensate.)

7. How has this benefited your life? What special gifts and talents have you developed for believing this lie? What are you known for being exceptional at? You have certainly achieved some skills because of needing to compensate for feeling like a failure in the other area.

8. Make a statement of the truth (Declaration of Truth!) You don't have to compensate anymore. You can choose to see and act upon the "truth" of the matter, (i.e. I am…)

   Practice your statement. You can transform your life no faster than you can get honest. Don't expect your pattern to change overnight. It requires practice. Attempting to stop your pattern only makes it worse. Accept it, appreciate what it has done for you, and own it!

Here is one of the games I used to play:

1. My Pattern: Relationships with men cause pain. Fear of intimacy.

2. My Perpetration: Men use and abuse me.

3. The Payoff: I avoid intimate relationships. I avoid intimacy so I can be right. I have proven myself right.

4. The Cost: My health, happiness, loneliness, feeling unloved, not having a companion, and depression.

5. Is It Worth It? No, the cost is too great!

6. My Compensation for Believing the Perpetuation: Going within spiritually takes me away from relationships with men, so I don't have to deal with abuse and intimacy.

7. The Benefit: I focused my attention on my spiritual growth.

8. Declaration of Truth: I am a valuable, caring, loving, intimate, spiritual woman who is open and feels safe to receive love. I experience inner peace. I have a loving, nurturing, supportive, intimate relationship with a wonderful man who respects, appreciates, and accepts me for who I am.

Once the mind sees the game, it can respond in truth. This may require time to support and re-program the mind to end the former pattern. When you realize you are paying too much (cost) for what you get back (your compensation), your mind supports you to *"tell the truth."*

When you really look at your life actions, behaviors, words, and thoughts, and realize the truth, a healing can occur. Also, you no longer play the "victim" and instead become responsible for your life choices.

꙳   ꙳

Stop ALL Shoulds and Trys!

Should is a powerful word. *Should* is a word that can damage and encourage you to make wrong choices. Many emotions are tied up in the word *should*, such as blame, guilt, and anger. *Should* is a word that beats you up. Who said you have to be perfect? Whose standards or *shoulds* do you attempt to live up to? Your own or someone else's? In other words, to whom do you strive to prove yourself–your spouse, mother, father, boss, friend, society, church? The *shoulds* are non-acceptance of who you are.

Below are examples of how people use *should:*

- ❖ Blame = It is your fault, you *should* have listened to me.
- ❖ Guilt = I *should* have never gotten involved.
- ❖ Anger = I *should* have gotten that raise, not them.
- ❖ Guilt = You *should* go visit your mother.

When the word *should* is used, your power and freedom are taken away and you no longer have a choice. By using the word *should,* you are saying you are wrong and you become a victim.

Think for a moment–can you live up to your *shoulds* and maintain perspective? Perhaps it is time to be conscious of your *shoulds* and eliminate them from your vocabulary.

In *Loving What Is*: *Four Questions That Can Change Your Life*, Byron Katie states, "In reality, there is no such thing as a 'should' or a 'shouldn't.' These are only thoughts we impose onto reality. Without the 'should' and 'shouldn't,' we can see reality as it is, and this leaves us free to act efficiently, clearly, and sanely."

The word *try* is another word to notice in your own vocabulary and in how other people use it. When someone says they will *try*, usually nothing happens, because they don't commit. Be concrete in your words. Instead of saying "I will *try*," be definite one way or the other–decide rather than deflect. You don't *try* to pick up the pen, you either do or you don't.

I learned a quick way to stop using the word *try* from Clinton Swain's Frontier Training Workshops. Every time you use the "*T*" word in his training, you owe $10 and the money goes to the orphans he sponsors. At home, when I use the "*T*" word I put a dollar into a jar. At the end of the month I give the money to my favorite organization, charity, or homeless person. This helps me to be conscious of my words, and it is a win for everyone.

Emotional Clearing

Years ago, I began to work with emotional clearing. It is a visualization process which easily allows your sub-conscious mind to go back in time to various situations that have been controlling you in some way. You will be the adult, rescuing the child or adolescent.

It is important that you, as the adult, say what needs to be said. Perhaps there are thoughts and feelings you weren't able to express when you were younger.

Once you have embraced the child or adolescent and they feel safe, comfortable, and secure, you may feel a sense of inner peace. Below is the process I use for emotional clearing:

1. Allow yourself to be in a comfortable position. Gently close your eyes.

2. Ask yourself to set aside fears, concerns, and ego so the truth can be revealed.

3. Take a deep slow breath through your nose. Hold it to the count of three. Exhale and let out a sound. Take another deep breath, breathing in peace. As you exhale, let go of any tension and anxiety, and allow your body to relax. As you take one more deep breath, let your mind become still as you exhale. You came to rescue your child or adolescent.

4. Imagine, visualize, or sense a long corridor in front of you. Notice there are a lot of doors on both sides of the corridor. The doors may or may not be different sizes, shapes, and colors. Take a deep breath and slowly walk down the corridor. Feel safe as you walk past different doors. Continue to pass doors until you feel drawn to a certain one. It doesn't matter what side of the corridor it is on.

5. As you stand in front of the door, notice how you feel. Notice the door size, the shape, and the color. What body sensations do you feel as you stand in front of the door? Now place your hand on the doorknob and notice any new sensations you feel in your body.

6. Slowly open the door, look inside, and notice who is there. What is the child or adolescent doing? How old does the child or adolescent look? Who is with them? What is being said or done? As you look at the child or adolescent, what expression do you see on his or her face?

7. Slowly go over to the child/adolescent and tell them you are here for them and you are going to care for and protect them. Notice how you feel in your body as you say these words. Now look at the reaction of the child/adolescent as they hear your words. Tell them you are sorry you didn't come sooner.

8. As the adult, say whatever you desire to the people in the scene. Say things you weren't able to say when you were a child/adolescent. Notice how you feel in your body when you speak your truth.

9. When you feel complete, take the child/adolescent by the hand, or hold them in your arms, and tell them that the

53

two of you are going to leave and you are going to a nicer place. Promise you are going to take care of and protect them.

10. Hold the child's/adolescent's hand, or carry them in your arms, and begin to walk out of the room. Don't look back. When you get outside the door, close it tightly and leave the corridor.

11. When you leave the corridor, embrace your child/adolescent, and express your love to them. Assure them you are always going to be there. Let your inner child know you are going to have fun times together and you will listen to what they need. Notice how you feel and the expression on the child's/ adolescent's face.

12. Ask them if they want to tell you anything. Listen to what they say to you. Ask them what they need from you. If you can give them what they really need, tell them you will make sure it happens. Thank the child/adolescent for trusting you and coming with you.

13. Embrace the child/adolescent again and tell them you love them. As you hold your child/adolescent, sense, visualize, or imagine they are merging into the center of your heart. Notice how you feel.

14. Now you can continue to walk down the corridor until you are drawn to another door and repeat the same process as above, where you will discover another situation. Or you can come back and do this process another time. Do whatever feels comfortable to you.

15. When you feel complete, notice how you feel. Take a deep breath and walk back to the entrance of the corridor.

When you reach the end take another deep breath. Notice the sounds around you. When you feel comfortable gently open your eyes.

Enjoy the magical times that come your way!

Voice Dialogue

I have used voice dialogue for decades as part of my healing and to gain valuable insight into various situations. I use this exercise when it feels like a battle is going on inside my head, when part of me feels one way and another part of me feels different and I cannot decide what to do or how to change a situation.

Numerous times it would be about intimacy. I wanted it, yet another part of me didn't want to have anything to do with intimacy. So I had to find out what voice or sub-personality within me didn't want intimacy and the reasons. I had to discover if it was Little Sharon, the teenager, the nun, the protector, or someone else fighting with the adult Sharon.

Once I knew who it was, I had a conversation with her, exploring the situation. The dialogue went back and forth until we came up with a happy solution for both of us.

You can also use voice dialogue to solve a variety of situations.

- ❖ When I feel like I am being pulled in two different directions, I need to separate the voices. I take the time to really listen to each voice within my head using the chair-to-chair process.

  This is a fun exercise. It is like working with your sub-conscious mind—feel vs. think, good self vs. bad self, child vs. adult.

Chair-to-chair process:

1. Set up two chairs facing each other, a comfortable distance apart. One chair is for you to sit in and the other chair is for the circumstances, other person, feeling, or situation.

2. Sit in your chair and say whatever you need to say.

3. Move over to the other chair and respond to what you heard being said.

4. Continue to move back and forth between chairs. You will be amazed at the answers, responses, suggestions, and comments you receive from the other chair.

5. Once you come to a perspective where you can resolve the conflict and come up with a solution, you can make positive choices.

Have fun with the exercise and let the voices that are holding you back find peace.

❧ ❧

DABDA

When I first became infected with HIV (known then as ARC – AIDS Related Complex), I attended several seminars where the late Elisabeth Kubler-Ross, MD presented. She was an amazing woman, full of love, compassion, humor, and understanding. She talked about death and dying and introduced the meaning of DABDA, explaining how everyone faced with a life-challenging illness or death goes through the five stages. The following explains this acronym and how it applied to my life:

D = Denial—When I was first diagnosed with HIV, I went into denial. I admitted the truth about my infection to my sister, Joyce, my boyfriend, Sid, and my minister, and that was all. I was already working in the AIDS community and had never met another infected woman. I thought nothing would happen to my health.

A = Anger—Anger set in when I started to get symptoms associated with HIV/AIDS, such as extreme fatigue, night sweats, wasting syndrome (severe weight loss), diarrhea, and memory loss. At this point I was angry and could no longer believe nothing could happen to me. The fact was I could get AIDS complications and die from them.

B = Bargain—Yes indeed, I bargained with Infinite Spirit. "If you make me well, I will serve you in whatever way you want me to. I will also take better care of my mind, body, and spirit."

D = Depression—I went into deep depression. I could no longer do some of my activities. At one point, my daughter, Jeaneen, became the mother and I became a child.

A = Acceptance—Once I embraced the fact I was infected, I was able to speak my truth and share my experiences with others. Acceptance allowed me the strength to move forward in a powerful way, but I had to go through all of the stages to get to empowerment and acceptance. Then I experienced peace.

At some point of illness or facing death, a person will go through the stages of denial, anger, bargaining, depression, and acceptance. From time to time, they may even jump back and forth between stages. However, when acceptance is embraced, peace of mind can dwell within.

Once I understood the meaning of DABDA, the five stages I would go through, I was able to understand what stage I was in and what I needed to go through in order to move onto the next step. Acceptance was my goal—yet it took time.

Grief

Grief is one of the hardest chapters to write—probably because I had such a hard time handling grief in the early part of my life.

There are two approaches to grief. You can avoid the pain and emotions associated with your loss and continue on, hoping to forget. Or you can recognize your grief and seek healing and growth. I have learned the hard way that healing can only begin when I give myself permission to feel–feel the pain, sadness, loss, and emptiness. The way out of grief is through it. There is no way around it.

It can take months and sometimes years to come to terms with the emotions around grief, before feeling a sense of peace and balance. From time to time, an event, a word, a song, or a thought may bring the loss back into your consciousness. In some situations, a person may never fully get over the pain of their loss.

Whatever emotion you are feeling at the time of your loss, it is important not to minimize your feelings. Coming to peace with the emotional chaos, loneliness, depression, pain, and confusion of grief is a process. Each person experiences grief differently. There is no right or wrong way to grieve. Grief is experienced internally and externally.

While going in and through grief, you may experience some of the following and more:

❖ Emotions—anxiety, sadness, shock, guilt, frustration, anger, and depression.

❖ Physical Sensations—low energy, breathlessness, tightness in chest and throat.

❖ Thoughts—confusion, disbelief, difficulty concentrating.

❖ Behaviors—insomnia, withdrawal, restlessness, shift in appetite, seeking comfort in spirituality, or perhaps turning your back on it.

There are various situations you may grieve about, such as:

1. The death of a family member or friend.
2. The death of a pet.
3. The loss of a job.
4. Aging losses.
5. The loss of a relationship.
6. The loss of your health.
7. Fire loss—personal items and home.
8. A move to a new location.
9. The end of a marriage or relationship.
10. Not being with your child(ren) due to divorce.
11. Your child(ren) leaving for college.
12. Loss of your identity due to a career change.
13. Loss of independence due to your health.
14. Loss of your dreams.
15. Natural disasters around the planet.

My loving friends Stephen and Ondrea Levine are well-known authors and presenters, and compassionate, loving people who for decades brought peace of mind to dying people. In Stephen's book, *Unattended Sorrows: Recovering from Loss and Reviving the Heart,* he writes, "We grieve the loss of love and loved ones;

experience fear, remorse, and the loss of trust in what may come next. And we grieve the tendency to mistake our pain for the truth, to think we deserve to suffer just because we are."

❖ My four major losses/griefs are each different, but they were profound and had their own journey of healing.

1.   When I was a child, my parent made one of our spare bedrooms into a doll house for me. I called this room, "My Special Place." My dad was a captain in the Navy and he hired a man on the ship to build me a stove, cupboards, refrigerator, sink, table, and chairs. My mom bought high chairs and cribs for my baby dolls. Susie was my favorite baby. I turned to her during my darkest times to talk about my sexual abuse. I could tell Susie everything. My mom decorated My Special Place like a real house with curtains and rugs. Mom, my babies, and I would have tea parties every day.

When I was 12, we moved to what my parents felt was a bigger, more beautiful home. This became a major loss in my life. I lost security within My Special Place and all of my doll accessories. Once we moved into our new house, Susie was no longer my companion, friend, or baby. She became just a doll. It was harder to lose My Special Place and my baby Susie than it was to move away from my friends in the neighborhood.

Whenever I expressed my sadness, loss, anger, and frustration over the loss of My Special Place, I was told to get over it, it was just a room. Behind closed doors, I cried in silence as tears rolled down my cheeks. My parents didn't understand the depth of my feelings and security I felt in My Special Place.

2. As I was growing up, my closest physical friend and hero was my brother Tommy. He was two years older than me. When I was 21, he was killed instantly in a motorcycle accident. When Tommy died, part of me died! I wasn't allowed to grieve his death. I couldn't find comfort with my family, because they had disowned me (for a year) when I divorced my husband, Tom, for a Chinese man. The man I left Tom for was abusive and wouldn't allow me to express my feelings, or talk about my how important Tommy had been in my life. The intense pain and loss was stuffed deep within me, and it took nearly 20 years to heal.

3. My third major loss was when I became sick due to AIDS complications. My daughter Jeaneen became the mother and I became the child. I grieved for the loss of my independence and the burden I felt I put upon people. I grieved and longed for all the amazing times Jeaneen and I had together. I grieved for the joy of being a mother and friend to my daughter's friends. I also grieved the loss of so many friends who turned their backs on me when they discovered I was infected.

4. Another very serious form of grief I had to work though is what some refer to as "survivor's guilt." In the mid-1980s to early 1990s, I lost many dear friends (men, women, and children) due to AIDS complications. I felt guilty I lived and they didn't. My heart still gets heavy when I think about how they suffered. I questioned: Why not me? Why am I still alive? Why did almost all of my friends die and I lived? Then I learned it wasn't for me to question. I needed to accept I am right where I am supposed to be, doing what I am doing, moment by moment. I also realized it was important for me to stay healthy so I could keep their loving memories alive.

I didn't experience the full impact of my grief until the initial shock of my loss and the numbness that came with it began to fade.

Someone wrote, "We honor the fact that we will never 'get over' our loss. Hopefully, we'll find that we don't need to 'get over it.' We may even find that our grief and loss have been transformed into a very precious gift."

In the book, *Who Dies?: An Investigation of Conscious Living and Conscious Dying*, Stephen and Ondrea Levine write, "When we turn toward our pain instead of away from it, self-mercy enters those parts of ourselves we had closed off, withdrawn from, or abandoned to feelings of importance. When it seems there is nowhere else to turn, when all our prayers and strategies seem to be of little avail, something deeper arises: a mercy that leads toward the heart."

So how does one cope with grief, regarding death? I would like to share some of my methods:

- ❖ Forgive myself for all the things I believed I *should* have said or done before Tommy died.

- ❖ When I was depressed with the loss of Tommy, I realized I wasn't taking care of myself. I didn't eat regular meals, exercise, or get out to visit people or places. Instead, I was hibernating deep within my own isolation. I learned to maintain a balanced lifestyle.

- ❖ I learned it was important to find supportive people I could talk to about my feelings and emotions.

- ❖ As a way to communicate my thoughts and emotions, I wrote, and wrote, and wrote.

❖ Grief is exhausting. I learned to listen to my body and when it needed a break, I would relax and rest.

❖ I lit a candle and placed it on an altar in memory of the person.

❖ On my altar I placed photos, mementos, and other items which represented the person.

❖ I planted a flower or tree in memory of the person.

❖ I honored the anniversary of their transition in a special way and shared stories about our times together.

❖ When I became sad and lonely for the person, I talked to his or her Spirit and listened for his or her loving voice.

❖ I used ritual as a means of healing.

Pets are family members, and for some people they consider their pets their children. The loss of a pet can be as deep as the loss of a human, because the heart knows no difference between a human and a pet. When your special pet dies, it is important to grieve and not allow people to make you feel foolish about your grief. If you have a pet and you have to put them to sleep you may want to think about doing some of these things:

1. Thank your pet for all the joy and love they brought you.

2. Take off their collar and name tags and keep them.

3. If you have another pet, you may want to take the healthy pet to say goodbye, so it can sniff, smell, or lick your ill pet before it dies.

4. If you feel comfortable, hold your pet in your arms as they are given the shot.

5. If your pet is cremated or buried, you may want to do a ceremony.

6. You may want to set up an altar, place special things on it, and light a candle.

7. Plant a tree in memory of your pet.

8. Make a donation to an animal shelter.

Know that there is no magic time for getting over your grief. You have a right to feel the loss in your heart and celebrate the life of your pet or loved one in whatever way feels comfortable to you.

Everyone encounters grief. It is of the utmost importance to honor it. Know it is real and seek out whatever method of healing is appropriate. Know you are not alone. My heart goes out to you as you embrace your grief.

ช่อ   ด่ว

Your Legal Affairs

Peace of mind is priceless and when you have your legal affairs in order, your loved ones and you can have peace of mind.

Whether you are in optimum health or facing illness (*dis-ease*), it is important to have all your legal affairs in order to prevent the government from walking away with the little or large amount you have. More importantly, you then have the final say if you want to be kept alive, especially if you are terminally ill or in a coma.

I remember when my doctor gave me six months to live in 1987, I got all of my legal affairs together: my living will/advance health care directive, power of attorney, and my will. Many years have passed, and I have since updated information on some of the matters.

Below is a brief description of the necessary legal documents you may want to get in order. You can go to the National American Bar Association website to find extended definitions and explanations at http://www.abanet.org/rppt/public. Each state has its own regulations and laws.

❖ A Power of Attorney is a written document signed by you giving another person power to act on your behalf to conduct your business. A Power of Attorney can be: a) general power of attorney, which covers all activities, and b) special power of attorney, which grants powers limited to specific matters, such as selling a particular piece of real estate, handling some bank accounts, or executing a limited partnership agreement in your name.

❖ A Living Will, also known as a Power of Attorney for Health Care or Advance Healthcare Directive, is a document authorized by statutes in all states in which you appoint someone as your proxy or representative to make decisions on maintaining extraordinary life-support if you become too ill, are in a coma, or are certain to die. You can also state in your Living Will if there are certain people you do or do not want to have visit you.

❖ A Will is a written document which leaves your estate to your choice of any named persons or entities. If you don't have a will at the time of your death, your estate will pass by interstate succession according to the laws of the state where you die.

❖ A Trust is a legal entity which continues to exist after your death. Thus, property transferred to your trust before your death will pass according to your instructions in the trust without the need for probate. This can save a lot of time and expense, particularly if you own a home at the time of your death.

❖ Domestic Partners. If you share the same residence with a person you consider to be your partner, there are some states, such as California, where there is a law that surviving registered domestic partners will have all the rights of a surviving spouse following the death of the other spouse.

A registered domestic partnership may be established by two persons who are at least 18 years of age and either a) both persons are members of the same sex or b) if the persons are of opposite sexes, at least one of them must be over 62.

To establish a registered domestic partnership, the two persons must file a Declaration of Partnership with the Secretary of State. Merely living together doesn't create a domestic partnership.

Many members of the gay and lesbian community have heard they have additional rights, including the right to control disposition; however, it is likely that a significant number of them don't realize they can obtain these rights only by filing a Declaration of Partnership with the Secretary of State. For more information, please contact your Secretary of State department.

❖ You may also want to take the time to write an Ethical Will. This is not a legal document, but more like a personal letter. In your Ethical Will, you can share your values, blessings, life's lessons, hopes, and dreams for the future, as well as love and forgiveness with your family, friends, and community.

If you don't have your legal affairs in order, now might be the time to do so, because you never really know the time of your last breath.

ॐ   ॐ

Mapping Your Way to Your Heart's Desire

Treasure mapping or creating a vision board is a fun, creative process that gets you out of your head and allows your heart to speak to you. I do this visual process every few years. Whatever you desire—a relationship, a home, a job, traveling, a car, optimum health, money, or anything else—you bring it into manifestation quicker as you become clear about what you truly desire. Seeing your heart's desires on paper will help them become reality.

Decide what you desire. You can make a treasure map or vision board about one particular goal, or include different aspects of your life. Recently I completed a treasure map for the next five years, which includes photos to represent laughter, playfulness, meditation, a new home, close relationships, traveling around the world for work and pleasure, my books published and on the *New York Times* bestseller list, speaking in front of large audiences with standing ovations, being on *The Oprah Winfrey Show* again, enjoying nature, receiving an honorary doctorate degree, optimum health and fitness, being of service to Infinite Spirit and humanity, and financial security.

It is fun to get a group of close friends together and have an afternoon set aside to create your vision board.

❖ Below are the steps I use:

> 1. Collect stacks of magazines, (kinds that apply to what you want to manifest), and look through them. Notice which pictures and phrases resonate

with you. Which pictures are you drawn to? What words or phrases speak to you?

2. Do not question your choices. Just rip out the pictures and phrases and set them aside. The miracle about treasure mapping is you don't need to know where the desired objects or opportunities will come from.

3. Before long you will have a lot of items.

4. After you have ripped out all the pictures and phrases in the magazines or catalogs you were drawn to, create one pile for goals you definitely want to manifest and a second pile for items you can live without.

5. Get a large sheet of poster board or construction paper (colored or non-colored) for backing your pictures.

6. From your first pile, set your images on your paper in whatever way you are drawn. Then take pictures from your second pile and incorporate whatever you want onto your vision board. Look at the way you have placed your pictures and phrases before pasting them onto the paper.

7. The visual appearance is powerful, so you don't want too many phrases included.

8. When you feel peaceful and empowered as you look at your treasure map, begin to paste your special pictures and phrases onto the paper.

9. Now as you look at your completed vision board, notice how you feel. What is it telling you?

10. Before you is what your heart desires. Now be open to receive it. You have pictured that which you desire, and through your photos and phrases, that vibration will resonate out into the world and draw what is for your highest good.

11. You may choose to practice a ritual or say a prayer after you have completed your treasure map. Give thanks for this or something better.

12. You may find it useful to laminate your vision board and place it on a wall where you can view your dreams every day.

Feng Shui (pronounced fung shway) is another way to lay out the design of your treasure map or vision board. Below is a general description of the layout from top to bottom, left to right. Divide your paper into nine equal squares and place your pictures and words according to the category of the box. If you decide to use Feng Shui for your treasure map, you can put a splash of color into it. Use the colors listed if your pictures don't have enough of the colors in them. The last treasure map I created I used Feng Shui.

People who have used Feng Shui to arrange their home, offices, or to create a relationship, have had a lot of success. I have used Feng Shui in my home in the placement of my furniture, plants, candles, crystals, mirrors, metal chimes, and bells.

There are numerous books on the market about the various ways to use Feng Shui. Below is a general layout I have used:

Rear Left

Prosperity,
Abundance
Colors: Purple,
Red
"Gratitude"

Rear Middle

Fame, Reputation

Color: Fire Red

"Integrity"

Rear Right

Relationships,
Love, Marriage
Colors: Pink, Gold,
Red, White
"Receptivity"

Middle Left

Family
Colors: Green, Blue

"Strength"

Center

Health
Colors: Earth
Tones, Yellow
"Earth"

Middle Right

Creativity, Children
Colors: White,
Pastels
"Joy"

Front Left

Knowledge,
Skills, Wisdom
Colors: Black,
Dark Green
"Stillness"

Front Middle

Career, Life Path

Colors: Black,
Dark Tones
"Depth"

Front Right

Helpful People,
Travel
Colors: Gray,
Black, White
"Synchronicity"

The above layout is similar to the Bagua.

Use your imagination. The Universe will match it!

Bach Flower Essences

During my healing process I benefited from using Bach Flower Essences. These plant and flower-based formulas can help manage the emotions by bringing negative attitudes and feelings back into balance and perspective. Bach Flower Essences help to restore and maintain emotional balance, free the body's own healing functions, and promote overall wellness.

There are 38 Bach Flower Essences divided into seven different categories:

1. Fear
2. Loneliness
3. Over-care for welfare of others
4. Despondency or despair
5. Uncertainty
6. Over-sensitivity to influences and ideas
7. Insufficient interest in present circumstances

Within each of the categories are many individual essences to choose from. Each essence has a specific description and benefit. Bach Flower Essences are 100% natural spring water infused with a wildflower by a sun-steaming method or boiling. The essences are based in 27% alcohol. Grape brandy, the most natural preservative, is used to preserve the spring water from going stagnant.

Here are the recommended ways to take the Bach Flower Essences:

❖ Add 2 drops of your chosen essence to a glass of water and sip at intervals. Repeat as necessary until the desired effect is achieved.

❖ To combine several essences, a Bach 30 ml mixing bottle is recommended. Your personal formula can then be carried with you.

Don't place the remedy in a plastic bottle. Use a dark shaded glass bottle (brown or blue) which can be purchased at most health food stores.

To combine essences, fill the mixing bottle to below the neck with spring water; add 2 drops of each chosen essence (maximum of 7), and take 4 drops of the mixture at least 4 times a day.

❖ The Bach Flower Essences can also be taken by placing 2 drops directly on the tongue, under the tongue, or rubbed onto the lips. You can also place the remedy behind the ears, on the temples, or on the wrists.

❖ It is important not to let the dropper touch your mouth, tongue, or skin, as this would contaminate the essences.

I keep the Bach Flower, Rescue Remedy, (in a bottle, spray, or cream form) in my medicine cabinet and purse. I experience immediate results with this remedy. You can take it for various reasons such as:

❖ Tension
❖ Trauma
❖ Impatience
❖ Emotional shock from an accident
❖ Heated arguments or startling experiences

❖ Calming the troubled mind before bedtime
❖ During childbirth – check with doctor before using
❖ Stressful situations such as exams, doctor or dentist appointments, and public speaking

If you use Rescue Remedy in the mixture, consider it as one essence, but use 4 drops.

Bach Flower Essences are safe for your pets—just add it to their drinking water.

For more information about Bach Flower Essences go to the website at http://www.bachflowers.com, or call Nelson Bach USA, Ltd. at 1-800-319-9151.

Aromatherapy

Aromatherapy is a modern word used to describe essential oils. Aromas have been used for over 3,000 years, created by burning plants and incense for ceremonies, meditations, and healing practices, and in oils and perfumes for beauty and pleasure.

Essential oils are most commonly steam-distilled extract from flowers, plants, weeds, stocks, roots, woods, and resins from around the world. Once extracted, an essential oil has a complex chemical composition which creates its healing nature.

Smell has a powerful effect on your body. Some smells might bring back pleasant memories, like the smell of homemade bread, fresh baked cookies, a loved one's fragrance, or cherry pipe tobacco. Other smells could bring up bad memories, such as the smell of alcohol on one's breath, the smell of a cigar, or hay. Certain smells evoke chemical reactions in the body.

There are various brands of essential oils, but the main one I use is Young Living. I have also used Aura Cacia, Simplers, Wyndmere, and NOW.

Young Living oils are from all over the world and the purest oils I have used. To learn about these oils visit www.youngliving.com.

Some of the ways you can use your essential oils are for massage, perfumes, diffusers, sprays, cleaning, therapeutic, and medicinal.

❖ Mix the essential oils in with your favorite oil, such as almond, jojoba, or olive.

❖ Add drops to your favorite non-scented cream or lotion.

❖ Add a few drops of your favorite essential oil into a spray bottle with good filtered water. I love to spray lavender around my bedroom area before I go to bed.

There are a lot of uses for aromatherapy. However, use caution. Not all oils are safe for all purposes. More information can be accessed in magazines, books, health food stores, and on the Internet to support the most positive experience.

Feel Loved

Throughout my years of healing I have encountered and participated in various processes that have made a profound difference in my life. I would like to share the following one.

During one of my weekend trainings with *Kalos Transformational Healing Programs,* we did the following exercise. One person stood in the middle and everyone made a large circle around the person. The one in the center kept their eyes open and people around the outside of the circle, one at a time, slowly and with open heart, looked into the person's eyes as they said the following supportive thoughts. Imagine how powerful it would be to hear these words spoken to you, and the feelings the words would bring up. Tears streamed down my cheeks as I embraced these words:

❖ I am glad you were born.

❖ You are beautiful in every way.

❖ We have looked forward to your birth.

❖ I love you.

❖ I will always love you no matter what you do.

❖ It is okay for you to say "no."

❖ I want to treat you with true love and affection.

❖ The problems in the family are not your fault.

❖ You don't need to try to fix the family marriage.

❖ You need to be a child.

❖ You can think your own thoughts.

❖ You can want what you want.

❖ I encourage your growth.

❖ It is okay to make mistakes.

❖ Mistakes help you learn.

❖ I am proud of you.

❖ I will stand by you.

❖ I will nourish your differences.

❖ I want you to live.

❖ I enjoy being with you.

❖ You are fun to be with.

❖ I will never leave you.

❖ It is okay to explore and you can ask for help.

❖ It is okay for you to be angry—I won't go away.

❖ I support you in learning to choose.

❖ I won't abuse you or hurt you in any way.

❖ I encourage you to explore your sexuality.

❖ No one is perfect.

❖ I thank you for who you are.

Now take a deep breath. Those words are healing. Embrace them and allow them to fill you with love and gratitude. You are a Magnificent Being!

❖ Another way you can feel loved is to make a list of all the ways you feel loved. What expressions, words, gestures, actions, and behaviors remind you that you are loved? Keep adding to your list. When you feel down and out, embrace the truth of who you are and the ways you feel loved.

Thank you for the bright light and love you truly are. I am glad you were born, and so is humanity! You make a difference, just being YOU!

Whole Mind

Some people function more out of their right mind or their left mind. The right mind (brain) is creative, experiential, and Divine essence. The left mind (brain) is linear, conceptual, and ego-based. What if you blended the two for a whole mind which would be a practical application of virtues?

Below is a chart a friend of mine, Rev. Roxie Hart, gave me. The words are not in any particular order. As you read over the chart become aware of what MIND you usually use, and incorporate the Whole Mind and Virtues.

<u>Right MIND</u>	<u>Left MIND</u>
Divine Nature	Ego
Child of God	Separate
Inner Knowing	Reaction
Intuition	Sensory-based
Wisdom	Rationalization
Trust	Doubt
Faith	Fear
Belief	Disbelief
Expectancy	Expectation
Mindfulness, Now	Past, Future
Presence	Aloneness
Freedom	Bondage
Abundance	Lack, Limits
Surrender	Sacrifice
Connected	Individual

Whole	Broken
Perfect	Flawed
Powerful	Helpless
Order	Randomness
Infinite	Unworthy
Eternal	Chaotic
Exploration	Analysis
Namasté	

WHOLE MIND

Peace
Serenity
Grace
Ease
Awareness
Integrity
Joy
Beauty
Prosperity
Guidance
Gratitude
Delight

VIRTUES

Choice
Attention
Understanding
Discernment
Knowledge
Compassion
Acceptance
Calm
Generous
Gracious
Empathic
Forgiving
Appreciation
Allow
Forthright
Honest
Respectful
Kind
Detached
Creative

❧   ❧

Books with Study Courses & Workshops

1. *A Year to Live:*
   How to Live This Year as If It Were Your Last
   by Stephen and Ondrea Levine

In March 1997, I had a near-death experience (NDE) due to AIDS complications. A few years later, I joined a group of men and women from church to undertake a year-long project that changed people's lives forever. During the entire course, we lived as if it were our last year to live. Stephen and Ondrea's year-long program of strategies and guided meditations helped us complete things as we "practiced dying."

Some people in our group were healthy and others were facing health challenges. However, we all came together to start living our lives to the fullest, moment by moment, discovering what was important and what we needed. Then we consciously chose to let go of that which no longer served our well-being. We had an opportunity to complete unfinished business, examine our priorities, and place them in order. Several people left their jobs and started doing work they had always wanted to do. Many men and women made changes in their relationships—left them or became more committed. Some people found new ways to take care of their health and well-being. Everyone looked at their friends and loved ones differently, and embraced them from the wholeness of their hearts. A sense of inner peace entered our hearts and minds as we embraced death. It allowed us to embrace life, moment by moment.

Our lessons included "Forgiveness," "Letting Go of Control," "Gratitude," "Soft Belly Meditation," "Disposing of the Corpse," "Writing Your Obituary," and much, much more. Some faced their fears about death, and as the months passed they no longer feared it, but truly embraced death.

Through Stephen and Ondrea Levine's book *A Year to Live,* everyone in the group came to understand the importance of preparing for their own death in order to embrace their life more fully and consciously. As I shared my near-death experience (NDE) it also assisted the men and women to let go of their fears of dying.

The late Elisabeth Kubler-Ross wrote, "Stephen's work restores the heart and clears the mind—it offers an opening which even death cannot close."

Now, take a deep breath. Hold it to the count of three and exhale. Deep from the center of your heart, ask yourself—Am I ready to embark upon a journey that will change my life forever? If so, the year-long program, *A Year to Live*, is for you. Make sure you have support you can turn to, be it a friend, loved one, clergy, or therapist. A lot of emotions will come up, and you may need someone to talk to that can help you through the process. If you decide to join a group, the leader will also be there for you.

2. *Family Constellation Workshop*
Taught by Claus Kostka from Germany

There is an old Yugoslav saying that goes something like this: "When the grandfathers eat sour grapes, the grandsons drink sour wine." Out of our love for our parents we unconsciously take on their suffering, believing that doing so would actually relieve them. Though our intention is to give relief, this human tendency to want to sacrifice ensures the continuation of suffering from one generation to the next. According to Bert Hellinger, developer of Family Constellation Work, *blessings* are meant to flow from parent to child, not *suffering*.

Family Constellation Work began in Germany some 30 years ago by renowned psychotherapist Bert Hellinger. Prior to developing this approach to family resolution, he worked intimately with the Zulu tribes of Africa. Hellinger observed what he understood to be "group conscience" (also referred to by Carolyn Myss as "tribal conscience"). Within the framework of the "group conscience," the tribes remained in balance and harmony through the facilitation of the elders. Using principles of justice, love, and respect, the natural flow of love in the tribal lineage is available to all. In this way each tribal member lives an authentic life.

In the West, our tribe is our family. In the workshop, each participant has the opportunity to affirm their heart's desire. The ultimate question is: what is keeping one from creating their heart's desire in his or her life? The answer can be found in the "family conscience." Using these same principles of justice, love, and respect, this work resolves entanglements that are affecting generations today.

Behind the suffering there is the motive of love. In witnessing such pure intent and the pain that has been caused from entanglement, we experience compassion and respect for our ancestors. We give them their dignity by accepting what is. We honor them by letting go of the need to fix anything for them. As a result, the power, joy, and gifts that are hidden in our family lineage flow into our lives. From there we can make new choices and let go of the old ways.

Don't worry--there is no need to drag your whole family to class! The workshop is for the individual and is not traditional family group therapy. This work is a subtle, non-intrusive approach to resolving one's suffering without the rehashing of old wounds.

I was blessed to participate in several Family Constellation Workshops with internationally-renowned therapist Claus Kostka, who studied under Bert Hellinger in Germany, and has been in practice over 20 years. Claus practices in Germany and visits the states annually to hold workshops. His work is a source of deep heartfelt change in the lives of participants.

This is an account of one of my experiences:

❖ The Family Constellation Workshop was different than anything else I had ever heard of. My mind couldn't quite grasp it, but my Spirit knew I had to experience the quick and easy way to break destructive cycles without pain, blame, shame, guilt, or suffering. I leapt at the opportunity to learn more.

At the workshop, I expressed my heart's desire to Claus and the group, which was to have the strength and health to fulfill my life purpose. Claus then asked me to choose representatives among the workshop participants to stand in for certain members of my family, including myself. After placing each person, I sat down and watched the constellation unfold.

I was amazed how objective this process is. The representatives felt and took on the posture and personality of my family, without knowing any details. With few words spoken, movement and energy shifted right before me. I could observe the suffering and misunderstandings, and "look at it" without "being in it." Walls between members of my family began to dissolve, and I witnessed the love that has always been underneath.

As the process unfolded, I found it easier to breathe and felt my chest expand. I realized I no longer had to carry this family burden of suffering. I now embrace my entire lineage with love and respect. I no longer hold onto judgment, hate, or resentment toward any of my family. Love truly heals!

As a representative in other constellations, I viscerally stepped into the feelings and knowing of the family members I was representing. The human experience is more common than we think. What I have seen happen in the Family Constellation Workshops is each participant felt, understood, and witnessed something that reflected a part of their life which was being healed effortlessly.

After this workshop I noticed a profound shift in my relationship with men. I experienced a deep healing and love for my younger brother, Raymond, who is deceased. I have renewed self-confidence. I am able to be myself naturally and with ease. I now accept my role and place in my family lineage and take responsibility for my life and well-being. I experienced we are all connected. I am inspired to express myself again, and a burning desire to complete my books and get them published is rekindled. I embraced a new sense of inner peace as an underlying depression lifted. More than anything, I am experiencing a deeper compassion, love, and understanding for my entire lineage as I reclaim and unite my family within.

For information on Family Constellation Workshops facilitated by Claus Kostka in the United States and Europe, please e-mail familyconstellation@yahoo.com, or click on the British flag for English at http://www.clauskostka.de.

3. *The AIDS Mastery Workshop*
   Taught by Sally Fisher, Co-Founder of Northern Lights
   Alternatives

In 1986, when men were dying due to AIDS complications, a talented, compassionate, loving, humorous woman, and amazing friend of mine by the name of Sally Fisher, created The AIDS Mastery Workshop in New York at The Actors Institute. Almost immediately afterward she co-founded Northern Lights Alternatives, an organization that produced the workshops in cities from New York to Los Angeles, and from Toronto to the United Kingdom. In 1989, I became a participant in her workshop, and in 1990, I trained and became one of The AIDS Mastery team leaders.

The AIDS Mastery Workshop is an intensive weekend experience which challenges the notion that the quality of life depends upon its circumstances or duration and puts forward the idea that the quality of life is determined by how we hold those circumstances. In the ever-changing landscape of HIV, the circumstances are constantly shifting. In The AIDS Mastery Workshop, those impacted by these changes can explore the possibilities of living full, rich, and empowered lives.

The workshop is designed to serve people living with HIV/AIDS, their loved ones, caregivers, or others directly affected by the force of the epidemic.

The AIDS Mastery is designed to give participants the tools to live empowered lives. HIV strips away the illusion of immortality and with it the fantasy that life's concerns can wait. The workshop offers participants the opportunity to face those concerns, explore reality, and see beyond the issues that stand between them and their well-being. The work includes exercises and conversations that will shift participant's perceptions of their past, allow them to become more fully present, and expand their sense of future. The workshop deals with the emotional, psychological, and spiritual needs engendered by HIV and examines relationship and behavior patterns, denial, childhood issues, self-value, death, sex, support, and whatever is needed to guide participants home to themselves. The AIDS Mastery is a compassionate, practical, and powerful call to action and a call to heart.

The AIDS Mastery will gather people impacted by HIV to share their experiences, to look at the possibilities that life holds, and to redefine their relationships to the epidemic and to themselves. Participants will be offered an opportunity to step boldly forward expressing their dreams, their fears, their vulnerability, and their power while identifying personal needs and personal strengths in a safe atmosphere where anything can be discussed.

Decades after Sally Fisher's dream of The AIDS Mastery Workshop, her vision still lives on. For information about The AIDS Mastery Workshops throughout the United States and the UK please contact the following people at their e-mail addresses:

- ❖ Alice in Upstate New York - ramstar@adelphia.net

- ❖ Rob Camiso in New York City - RCammiso@nyc.rr.com

- ❖ Ed Kubler in Houston, Texas - ejktexas@comcast.net

- ❖ Scott Frelick in Dallas, Texas - rscott@dallas.net

❖ Frank Johnson in Oklahoma City -
   frank-johnson@sbcglobal.net

❖ Dennis Siple in Los Angeles, California -
   dsiple@ca.rr.com

❖ Hana Jones in the United Kingdom -
   hanajones414@btinternet.com

4. *The Artist's Way: A Spiritual Path to Higher Consciousness*
   by Julia Cameron and Mark Bryan

Once I became reacquainted with my inner child, I found it easier
to be creative, express myself in all areas of my life, and also be
more spontaneous. I journeyed inward through creativity by
joining a group called *The Artist's Way*. This is a 12-week
program by Julia Cameron and Mark Bryan which, through
readings, exercises, writing, and discussions allows you to
recover your creativity. You work through various blocks,
including beliefs, fears, jealousy, guilt, self-sabotage, addictions,
and other inhibiting forces, and replace them with confidence,
imagination, and productivity. This leads you down a path
toward a more balanced life and personal fulfillment.

The Artist's Way is not about art, though you do create some. It is
more about discovering your creative force, expressing your true
self, identifying your dreams, and making plans to accomplish
them.

The course is set up so each morning, as soon as you wake up,
you write three pages of whatever comes to your mind without
stopping. This is called your *morning pages*, and it helps to
overcome blocks and self-destruction. It doesn't matter what you
write about, you just write without censoring.

There are weekly reading and homework assignments. I never thought homework could be so much fun and insightful. In the course I attended, everyone got exactly what they needed from the group through insights, support, letting go of the past, and embracing the future. As the men and women supported each others' goals, the goals were accomplished, or were well on their way to being accomplished, within the 12-week course.

Julia Cameron says, "The exercises are designed to help a reader glimpse his or her inner artist that has been buried alive under a mountain of negative conditioning."

5. *Vein of Gold: A Journey to Your Creative Heart*
   by Julia Cameron

A year after completing *The Artist's Way* and applying everything I had learned from the course, I joined a group of people to study Julia Cameron's book, *Vein of Gold*. This 12-week course included the same exercises as *The Artist's Way;* however, it also required a 20-minute walk every day.

The processes in *Vein of Gold* bring you to a deeper level of your authentic self. They involve inner play, growth, renewal, and healing. Some of the tools we used were writing, making treasure map collages, storytelling, witnessing events, and sound.

"A pilgrimage is a physical process," writes Cameron. "This means that the tools of *The Vein of Gold* will be more deeply felt, and therefore more deeply resisted, than the tools of *The Artist's Way*."

6. *The Mask Project*
   Taught by Ruth Eileen Dorn

In 1998, I participated in *The Mask Project*. Ruth Eileen is a talented friend of mine and she encourages creativity through group interaction and exploration. Students create masks by molding plaster gauze over their faces, adding structural elements, and then adorning the masks with an amazing collection of materials—paint, papers, fabrics, buttons, beads, and much more. During the process, mask makers explore their inner qualities through storytelling and guided imagery. The masks reveal, rather than conceal. It is a creative, spiritual, nurturing, joyful process, where the three-dimensional replica of a participant's face becomes a symbol of personal power. The class is based on the principles presented in *The Artist's Way* by Julia Cameron.

A few days before attending The Mask Project, I had a dream about what my mask was going to look like. The first day of the workshop when I was carrying supplies out of the car, the "perfect" feathers fell to the ground, drawing my attention to them. Then everything came together with ease.

The following is what I wrote about my finished mask, which is entitled My Authentic Self:

My Authentic Self

Look into my eyes. They are the open windows of my soul. Brilliant rhinestones surround my eyes, reflecting the beauty within and the magnificent splendor that encircles me. I feel my life is balanced, as shown by dividing my mask into three equal sections.

The radiant violet color symbolizes my deep spirituality and connection to all. Positioned at ear level is an elegant jeweled pin which signifies one's ability to receive Divine Guidance from the spirit realm. The large brilliant center jewel symbolizes God's love for all. Rectangular facets connecting the center jewel with small circular stones portray my union with the human kingdom and spirit realm. Strands of gold and clear silver beads represent my connection to the plant, animal, and mineral domain.

The brilliant blue area depicts my life purpose of communication. A beautiful, colored wing of pheasant feathers represents my freedom to express the creative self through words, poetry, painting, and writing. For me this is "telling the truth." Through my communication, I assist others on their journey to wholeness and oneness.

The center, which glows with harmonious gold, is my unification with Infinite Spirit, self, and all. Within lies Divine wisdom, truth, inspiration, compassion, understanding, and love that surpasses all space and time.

On the interior side of my mask are pictures of items important and close to me. These include nature with trees, flowers, mountains, and a lake; horses gracefully running through the lush green fields; a soaring eagle high above with clear visions from beyond; the Universe with its colorful rainbows, glorious sunsets, and sparkling bright stars; words of wisdom and inspiration; and most important, a picture of my compassionate and loving daughter, Jeaneen.

It has taken many years for me to experience who I am. A few unhealed illusions and emotions still remain and are eager to be healed. They appear on the front of the mask, as indentations on the tip of my nose.

My journey has been challenging, yet, through all my various experiences, it has allowed me to understand MY AUTHENTIC SELF. So with time, in every relationship, I will be capable of expressing my inner beauty, and then the mask and I will become one. Until then, I will behold this mask often and remember who I truly am.

The amazing part of being in The Mask Project is you don't need to be artistic. All you need is an open mind and an expansion of the heart. Through the meditation, or even perhaps your dreams, you will see what part of your soul and spirit wants to come forth and be expressed in your mask.

To learn more about The Mask Project please visit: http://www.themaskproject.net.

THE BODY

❧ ❧

What is the Body?

We are not our body. Our soul and spirit are so much more. Our body is the vehicle in which we live while on this earthly plane.

Our physical body works like a machine. The blood, lymph, nerves, muscles, and bones all have to work in the right order at the right time for us to stay in top function and health. A grandfather clock with its many dials, some big, some small, all moving at different speeds, has to work perfectly in harmony and balance with all its parts in order to keep accurate time. Our physical body works the same way.

The brain, spinal cord, and central nervous system work much like a computer. They send signals and store files based on information we put in there. Thoughts create our reality, so negative thoughts about the body such as, "I am too fat," create responses down to a cellular level. If we consistently tell our body it is too fat, our internal computer (the brain and central nervous system) processes the information and creates fat cells. We get fatter. Emotions act in a similar way and are even stored in the physical body when they are not fully felt or expressed. Unresolved emotions may result in illness or *dis-ease*.

We have a lot of energy bodies that surround the physical body (Spirit Chapter, sub-chapter "Auras.") This is great! The energy body is our first line of defense. It is our energy field that first receives and processes everything we come into contact with, all thoughts, emotions, and energetic and environmental influences.

Long before the physical body shows signs of illness or *dis-ease*, that imbalance has been sitting in our energy field. Most of us know what's in our energy field, even if we don't like to admit it. For instance, we know if we eat right, exercise right, have negative thoughts or unresolved emotions. All this information is in our energy field. We know it is there because we either have lots of energy and feel happy, or we have little energy and feel sad and depressed.

When in a state of balance and alignment, the whole of us (our energy bodies and our physical body) has the ability to process information and release what is not necessary or healthy for us. When we are out of balance, or the influence is too big and we are ignoring it (unresolved emotions, poor eating habits, unhealthy lifestyle), this pattern stays in our energy field and eventually makes its way to the physical body where we experience it as illness or *dis-ease.*

We need to help our bodies (bones, muscles, internal organs, the central nervous system, brain, and spinal cord) stay in harmony by keeping everything in proper alignment so the bodies can work perfectly. In addition to a healthy lifestyle, we may also need to receive regular body therapy/work such as massage, CranioSacral Therapy, Energy Medicine, or Acupuncture. These therapies and treatments help to keep our energy fields and our physical bodies in balance, alignment, and health.

Pain or discomfort is a "wake-up" call to let you know something is out of balance. Listen to the call. The human body is complex with the innate ability to heal itself when given the proper tools.

In The Body Chapter and sub-chapters are various healing techniques I have used and taught to heal the body.

Throughout the world, *Bodies: The Exhibition,* and also *Body Worlds & The Brain – Our Three Pound Gem* have been on display. I spent over four hours viewing and listening to audio about the various parts of the body. I learned more in those short hours than all my years of schooling. I believe every child would benefit from viewing the body, and perhaps then embrace the sacredness of their body and life. I was in AWE for days. I highly recommend this exhibit to all men, women, and children. We truly are magnificent, beautiful, and complex. For more information, visit http://www.bodiestheexhibition.com/bodies.html.

∂⌒　⌒ᕤ

Your Inner Child

One of the most valuable and insightful lessons I learned from Linda in my healing process was getting in touch with my inner child. Everyone has an inner child, whether they are aware of it or not. Carl Jung called it the "Divine Child," Emmet Fox called it the "Wonder Child," Charles Whitefield called it "The Child Within," and some psychotherapists call it the "True Self."

The inner child is the ambassador between the mind-body-spirit. I realized when writing this sub-chapter the inner child could be placed in The Mind, The Body, or The Spirit Chapter. I chose to place it here because of the inner child's playfulness, expression, and movement.

Some parts of the Child you might act out are:

- ❖ The Fearful Child
- ❖ The Disconnected Child
- ❖ The Abandoned Child
- ❖ The Responsible Child
- ❖ The Wounded Child
- ❖ The Spoiled Child
- ❖ The Playful Child
- ❖ The Neglected Child

Each has his or her own personality, and you may find one or more aspects of a child controls or enters your life more often than others.

Most people, unfortunately, grew up in dysfunctional or troubled families. Most of the trauma, hurt, or damage you experienced in your lifetime occurred during your childhood. During your early years, you were sensitive, vulnerable, and open. As a child faced with challenges, the way you may have coped was to block out the pain, deny the abuse, or disown the trauma. As a result, on a day-to-day basis, you are no longer in touch with part of yourself.

During my nine years of being raped, my inner child longed to be protected, nurtured, and loved. She was fearful of men and didn't know whom to trust or how. She didn't feel safe. She felt isolated and alone. She was all choked up inside, and wasn't able to tell the truth or express herself. She silently and repeatedly screamed HELP! She felt empty, fearful, confused, and depressed. My inner child was scared to death, and she wanted to die.

For you as an adult to feel whole, your inner child must be embraced and expressed. When this child-self is not allowed to be heard or acknowledged as real, a false or co-dependent self emerges. Then you begin to live your life as a victim, or a perpetrator, which comes from the same place—survival.

There are various techniques and processes I have used, and continue to use, with my inner child. First, I had to acknowledge she was there. Then I had to get to know her and gain her trust. Then it was important to listen to her and hear what she needed. The following is a visualization I use to assist people to get in touch with their inner child:

1. Find a comfortable place where you can relax and let go of any outside noises.

2. Gently close your eyes.

103

3. Ask to set aside any fears, ego, or concerns so you will hear and see that which is for your highest good in love and light.

4. Take a few slow deep breaths in through your nose and out through your mouth. With each breath allow yourself to feel at peace.

5. Imagine, envision, or see yourself walking down a path. Create the path any way you like. It might be leading into a meadow, forest, mountains, stream, or beach. All that matters is the path you walk down makes you feel happy, peaceful, and safe. Notice what you create on each side of the path. There might be a stream, flowers, rocks, birds, trees, or other things. Notice what scents you smell, what sounds you hear, and what you see.

6. Continue to walk down the path and notice in the distance a large old tree. As you walk toward the tree, notice there is a boy or girl sitting with his or her back to the tree. Look at the child and notice the expression on the face and the body language. Notice how you feel as you look at this child. This child is you. How old are you? Ask this child if you can sit down next to or in front of them. If you receive permission, thank the child for allowing you to sit down.

7. Ask the child what they are feeling. Acknowledge the feeling (such as sadness, loneliness, pain, anger). Ask them how long they have felt that way? What made the child feel this way? Ask the child what else they are feeling. What else do they want to tell you that they have never told you before? Ask the child what they need in order to begin to heal.

8. Tell the child you are sorry you weren't able to take care of them, but you are an adult now and you want to protect, comfort, care for, nurture, and love them. Look at the child and notice what their body language and face look like. What do you as the adult feel inside?

9. Ask the child if you can embrace them, and if so, notice how you feel as you embrace one another. Tell the child you love them and you promise to be there for them from now on.

10. Thank your child for getting your attention. Ask the child if they would like to come together with you. If they say yes, then see yourself embracing and merging into one. Know your inner child is now embraced in your heart and will continue to need you to take time to talk to them. Notice how you feel now that you have met your inner child.

11. If your child tells you they don't want to come with you, ask if you can come visit them often. Know once they gain your trust, they will merge with you.

12. Begin to walk back down the path you created. Notice how you feel now that you have connected with your inner child.

13. When you reach the end of your path, take a deep breath in through your nose and exhale through your mouth. Begin to notice the sounds around you. Slowly move your body. When you feel comfortable gently open your eyes.

Once I gained trust from my inner child, she told me what she felt and what she needed from me. She wanted us to talk and play. When I asked her what she wanted to play, she told me dolls and to go high on the swing. I promised her we would do both.

I went to the toy store, called forth my inner child, and asked her to pick out a doll she wanted us to play with, along with some outfits. As a child, playing dolls was my favorite activity. Now as an adult, once again, I find joy and happiness in playing with dolls. When my inner child tells me she wants to swing, I set a time to do it, and ask if that will be all right with her. Today you might find me at the park among the children, swinging up in the air, laughing, smiling, and leaning way back as I look up at the sky. There is so much inner peace and joy when I fulfill the needs of my inner child.

I have learned when your inner child says they want something, if you cannot provide it, let them know why. If you promise to do something like play ball, dance, color, play in the sand, or fly a kite, and you don't do it, your inner child will feel re-injured. The old wounds you have been healing will be re-opened. In your mind you can visualize doing the things your child wants to do and they will be happy. However, you will feel happier physically doing them.

❖ During one of my rebirthing sessions, I got in touch with the newborn baby within me. I heard my mother say, "She is so ugly" when she saw me. As an adult, I didn't know this story, so I asked my mom what I looked like when I was born and she said, "I thought you were ugly. You had long dark hair and big black eyes, and that was all I could see." I was sad to hear her say that, but what was more important was my baby within was hurt and held onto the thought, "I am ugly." As an adult I have heard many people say a new-born baby is ugly. How can that be?

At the time, I was attending one of Susan Forward's therapy groups, and it was recommended I work with the inner child. To heal this wound, I went to the toy store and bought a baby doll to represent my baby within. The doll has black hair and big black eyes. I brought the doll home and named her "Baby Sharon." I held her in my arms, talked to her, kissed her, told her how beautiful she was, rocked her in a chair, and treated the doll as if she truly was my baby. After I felt comfortable with Baby Sharon, I dressed her in the beautiful pink crocheted long gown my mother made for me when I was an infant. Having Baby Sharon wear this beautiful gown my mom made me was part of my healing process.

Today I still have Baby Sharon in my bedroom. She sits in the musical rocking chair my daughter Jeaneen had when she was young, along with a homemade teddy bear my friend, Lois, made for me while I was in the hospital. Every morning I acknowledge Baby Sharon. From time to time I hold her in my arms and find out how she is feeling and if there is anything she needs. I know through the years of working with my dolls it has helped me to heal my baby and inner child. The reality is the baby and inner child are integrated within my Being.

❖ Getting to know my inner child contributed greatly to my healing of anorexia. I was stuffed with emotions and couldn't express them. My inner child suffered greatly, and I needed to work with her on my anorexia.

❖ Reclaiming my inner child supports my creativity, spontaneity, passion, desires, choices, and life purpose. She is my soul spirit working in harmony for the betterment of my life and well-being.

When was the last time you really allowed your inner child to come out and play? Think for a moment about your childhood. What brought you joy? What did you look forward to doing? Perhaps when you were a child you liked to play dolls, play ball, swim, dance, swing, color, finger paint, play in the sand, throw a Frisbee, fly a kite, ride a horse, or climb a tree. I encourage you to take time out of your busy schedule within the next week and play! Whatever it was that brought you so much joy, do it for yourself again—not for your children or grandchildren, but for you—your inner child and you. It doesn't matter what you do, just enjoy it, have fun and play. Then notice how alive and happy you feel.

As a child, adolescent, or adult, if you enjoy(ed) coloring, there are several books by Susanne F. Fincher with sacred circle designs called mandalas. When I have a desire to color, be centered, uplifted, or receive spiritual guidance, I will sometimes color in Susanne's *Coloring Mandalas Book 2: For Balance, Harmony, and Spiritual Well-Being*. After coloring a sacred circle, I feel inner peace, harmony, and reconnected.

Susanne states, "A mandala is a circular design that grows out of the urge to know oneself and one's place in the cosmos. …Mandalas express completeness and invite us to experience ourselves as a whole being, an individual."

Allow your inner child the freedom to express his or her Spirit.

Stress Reduction

Stress comes in many forms: emotional, physical, work-related, psychological, relationship-triggered, environmental, and much more. Stress can play havoc on your mind, body, and spirit. Yet some stress is unavoidable. The key is to release stress so it doesn't undermine your well-being.

Stress can cause many problems including:

❖ Sleep problems
❖ Depression and isolation
❖ Difficulty in relationships
❖ Weight gain or weight loss
❖ Anxiety, nervousness, and irritability
❖ A weakened immune system and other health problems

There are countless ways to release stress. See which of these works for you.

❖ Perhaps you enjoy exercising. Use physical movement as a way to release stress. Walk in nature, jog, bike ride, lift weights, play ball, or stomp your feet. Maybe you prefer something more subtle, such as yoga, Tai Chi, or Qigong. Just move your body.

❖ If you feel a need to yell or scream, grab a pillow, place your face into it, and scream as loud and hard as you need to. You can also get in your car, close the windows and doors, and scream as loud as you want.

❖ Hitting something like a pillow helps release negative energy.

❖ Take a hot bath while listening to your favorite music, and surround yourself with soft lights or candles. Relaxation can release stress and make you feel regenerated.

❖ Friends and loved ones can be a source of strength when you are shattered or drained.

❖ Comfort and relaxation might be found in crafts such as painting, knitting, sewing, or building something.

❖ You may have to confront the issue or person you are stressed out about.

❖ Meditation, prayer, and journaling are other forms of stress reduction.

❖ A massage can help release stress.

❖ Laughter releases tension.

No matter where you are there are three techniques you can always count on to release your stress and restore composure:

1. Use your breath. Stop whatever you are doing and become conscious of your breath. Breathe in slowly through your nose, then exhale and let out a sigh. Take another deep breath and hold it to the count of three. As you exhale, let go of any tension, frustration, anger, anxiety—any emotion you want to release. Consciously become aware of your breath until you feel a sense of calm, inner peace, and warmth enter your Being. It is amazing how quickly you can relax using your breath.

2. Do several shoulder shrugs. When you move your shoulders up, down and around, you release a great deal of stress.

3. Think about what has you tense or frustrated and what you want to release. Stand up, put your arms down at your sides, and tightly close your fists. Feel the tension in your forearms and your triceps. With the arms still tight, squeeze your buttocks and feel your upper thighs tighten up, knees tense, your calves and feet tense up. Now close your eyes and mouth tightly and extend your jaw and neck. Feel the tension throughout your entire body. Hold it to a slow count of 10.

Then take a deep breath and as you exhale, shake out all of the tension in your body.

If you do this process two or three times in a row, not only will you release tension or frustration, but you will feel lighter, more open, and free.

I highly recommend purchasing Dr. Andrew Weil's *Mindbody Toolkit: Experience Self Healing with Clinically Proven Techniques,* which has two powerful audio CDs with breathing exercises, meditations, visualizations, and a set of cards.

Your Body Knows What It Wants and Needs

Your body is a complex and useful instrument which provides all kinds of information. Once you become attuned to your body, you will be able to do Muscle Response Testing (MRT), also known as Kinesiology, to determine what your body wants and needs.

I have used muscle testing since 1985 as a means to discover what my body needs. Your body holds all the answers and all the data needed to understand your problems. Ten years later, I learned the various Trigger Points to touch on the body while using MRT through Kalos Transformational Healing Programs, led by my wonderful friend, Valerie Seeman Moreton, N.D. You can use these trigger points to determine vitamin and mineral deficiencies, digestion problems, allergies, and imbalances in hormones, organs and blood sugar levels, and much more.

In Valerie Seeman Moreton's book, *Heal the Cause: Creating Wellness – Body, Mind & Spirit* she states, "Muscle testing is a way to communicate with the cellular level of your body in a non-invasive way. It is a simple, workable gauge that gives a reading on the inner functioning of your mind and body. Because of the interrelationship between the muscles, organs, brain, nerves and electrical system of the body, you can uncover information held on a sub-conscious level. MRT is an accurate and revealing procedure that you personally can put into practice with a very little amount of training."

Throughout the day I do muscle testing for confirmation.

Valerie recommends the following:

1. Remove all potential interferences to test the body's subtle electrical energy accurately: jewelry, crystals, metal bands, all watches, and glasses. Gold and silver worn at the same time can cause a short circuit of your electrical system, as do batteries. Crystals may interfere by causing each test to test strong. Eventually you can test to see if any of the objects is interfering with the test.

2. Don't stand under fluorescent lighting, or by any other source of electromagnetic radiation, such as a running microwave oven or television screen.

3. Balance the three major electrical circuits by rubbing the following three areas of your body—your clavicle bones, above and below your lips, and the end of your tail bone. This will align the energy flowing:

    a. Side to side
    b. Up and down
    c. Front to back

Circuit balancing ensures the electrical communication between the brain, nerves, and muscles works well for accurate testing.

A. Bilateral Circuit—Energy flowing from left to right sides of the body. To correct: Rub the clavicle bones at the base of your neck with your dominate hand, while your other hand is pressing over your navel to balance the energy moving from side to side of your body.

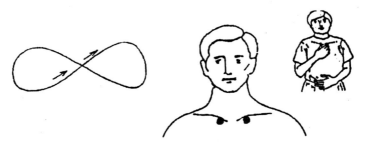

Bilateral Circuit

B. Lips Circuit—Energy flowing from top to bottom in the body. To correct: Rub above and below your lips with your dominate hand, while your other hand is held over your navel to balance the energy moving up and down in your body. While rubbing, roll your eyes in the direction of the vertical lazy 8, with your eyes going up at mid-point.

Lip Circuit

C. Coccyx (Tailbone Circuit)—Energy flowing from front to back in the body. To correct: Rub over the end of your tail bone with your dominant hand, with your other hand over your navel to balance the energy moving from front to back in your body. Roll your eyes in the direction of a flat

114

horizontal lazy 8 with you standing in the middle. Begin at your navel and move your eyes to your front left side, then around the back like butterfly wings. Bring your eyes through the middle of your body out the front right side and repeat the movement bi-laterally.

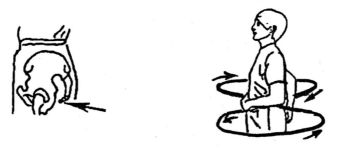

Coccyx (Tailbone) Circuit

With these three electrical circuits in balance, you are ready to being Muscle Response Testing.

Your body will respond strong to your true statements and weak to those not true. Strong means "Yes" and weak means "No." The muscles really do react to what you think, feel, or imagine.

Chiropractors refer to Muscle Testing as Applied Kinesiology, and some use it in their practice. Most chiropractors use the arm as a means of response. You stretch your dominant arm to the side, parallel to the floor. Then you have someone check your resistance by using their dominate hand to test. Press down on the arm (it doesn't have to be hard). The person being tested looks straight ahead, with eyes open. When you state a true fact, your arm will stay strong and perhaps rigid. When you make a false statement or are exposed to something your body doesn't want, your arm becomes weaker and drops. If you do a number of tests one after another, your arm will eventually become tired. You can switch to the other arm or rest for a moment.

Always remember to thank your body for your answers.

Before I start to do Muscle Testing, I always ask to set aside my ego, my concerns, and my fears so I can receive the truth that is for my highest good, or for the highest good of all concerned if other people are involved with my question. This will invoke the higher level of Truth.

Begin to use issues you know to be true or false so you can feel the difference in strong and weak responses. Use statements such as:

❖ My name is (state your true name). (Test) Then say my name is (state a false name). (Test)

❖ State one thing you like and then one thing you don't like. (Test both)

❖ Feel a positive emotion, such as joy or love. (Test) Then feel sadness. (Test)

❖ Mention a place you enjoy visiting. (Test) Then a place you dislike. (Test)

❖ State your favorite color to wear. (Test) Then your least favorite color to wear. (Test)

❖ Make up as many true and false statements you can think of until you become comfortable with the energy of both.

❖ When you are through Muscle Testing, thank your body for speaking to you through this technique.

Valerie states, "Never use MRT to make decisions for you. MRT is limited to what information has been stored in the memory banks of your body. You are the one to decide, not past programming. Never allow MRT to replace common sense. Be knowledgeable enough about what is 'normal' to question, if the testing seems strange. Use it to the extent you feel it is reliable and not when you are unsure. MRT is an art. The more you use it the better you become at it."

To learn more about Muscle Response Testing (MRT), the Trigger Points, and the Kalos Transformational Healing Programs or educational books go to http://www.kalos.org.

I also have used Muscle Testing the following way:

❖ Place your dominant hand on your heart chakra (center of your chest), and when you make a true statement your body will bend forward. When you make a false statement, your body will feel like it is being pushed backwards. You may not feel a big difference in the movement at first, but there will be some. If you find your body doesn't move forward and backward, but side to side, that is fine. The more often you practice this technique the stronger your response will become.

Always remember to thank your body for responding to your questions.

Before long, you will be able to hold any thought in your mind or object in your hand (herbs, foods, colors, or anything else) to see if your body desires it. If your reaction is weak, your body doesn't want it at this time. That doesn't mean it may not want it later. I test all of my vitamins and herbs every few months, including dosage amounts, and adjust them to what my body wants. When I test my prescriptions, I consult my doctor before changing the dosage.

Muscle Response Testing may feel frustrating at first, but the more you work with it, the quicker you can rely on the body to respond to yes and no or true and false questions.

Enjoy the process and have fun with it. This will allow you to become more conscious of what your body desires, needs, or wants. You may also use someone else's muscle (arm) to test which is a more objective test than using your own.

Before I started using muscle testing, I used a pendulum for information from my conscious and sub-conscious minds. There are many types of pendulums such as copper, teardrop, and crystal. You can even use a necklace with a pendant on the end. Below is a helpful guide to using a pendulum:

1. Hold a pendulum with your wrist slightly arched, and the string or chain three to six inches in length clasped between the forefinger and the thumb, so the pendulum has a downward drop. Separate your last three fingers so they can act as antenna.

2. Start by asking questions you know to be true or false, yes and no, so you can get used to the movement of the pendulum. For example, say "Higher Self, indicate the direction of Yes for me." Most people find either a forward and backward, or a clockwise direction indicates Yes. The opposite direction indicates No. If you find this is not true for you, go with whatever you experience when observing true or Yes statements.

3. Focus your intention on your question and say it aloud. Begin with questions or conditions where you aren't emotionally attached to the outcome.

4. If you have difficulty making the pendulum move consistently, consider the following: Are you forcing the situation? Are you tired? Are you in an imbalanced state? If so, then rest and work with the pendulum another time.

5. When you have finished asking questions with your pendulum, remember to always give thanks.

Dale Olson has a book entitled, *The Pendulum Charts: Learn to Access Your Natural Intuitive Abilities and Take the Guesswork Out of Life*. His spiral-bound book is filled with 44 various charts such as percentage/probability, time factor, quantity factor, supplements, remedies, relationships, and much more.

As with muscle testing, using a pendulum requires practice, persistence, and patience.

Body Dialogue

Your body has a voice, and when you quiet your mind, you can listen to what it needs.

Body Dialogue is a fun and interesting technique to discover where you hold emotions and what is needed for healing. Trapped emotions need to be released from the body. When you become conscious of where you store emotions, you can release them quicker.

I practice Body Dialogue every few months to discover what old emotions I have released, or what I still hold onto. Then I become conscious of new emotions I need to look at.

On the diagrams below, there are two bodies, one with a front view and one with a back view. There is no gender needed for this process. You have my permission to make copies of the larger body diagrams in the Appendix, located on pages 329 and 330, so you can compare your charts from time to time.

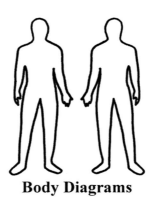

Body Diagrams

Listed below are several emotions. You can state any emotion you like, but here are some examples:

- ❖ Love
- ❖ Joy
- ❖ Happiness
- ❖ Gratitude
- ❖ Peace
- ❖ Fear
- ❖ Grief
- ❖ Anger
- ❖ Frustration
- ❖ Sadness
- ❖ Hopelessness

Look at the word, read it aloud, and then close your eyes and repeat the word. As you repeat the word, notice where you feel the emotion in your body. Do you feel a sensation on the front or back of your body? It doesn't matter what kind of sensation you feel: a twinge, warmth, cramping, tightness, expansion, or anything else. Once you locate the sensation, open your eyes and write the emotion on your body diagram exactly where you felt it.

After you write all of your emotions on your body diagram, see if there is one area you hold onto emotions more than another. Notice if the area in which you hold negative emotions is where you have pain or health problems.

Now that you have discovered where you hold your emotions (this will change as you heal), you can begin to dialogue with your body.

- ❖ Take a slow deep breath and quiet the mind. Then ask to set aside your fears and ego to hear the highest truth in love and light. One at a time, state the emotion and notice where you feel it in your body. Locate the exact spot. You can say the word aloud again. Then focus your attention (you may want to close your eyes) on the area in your body where you are holding onto the emotion. Ask the emotion to speak to you.

❖ Here is an example: You discover anger is located in the lower front part of your left arm, about two inches above your wrist. Focus your attention there and say, "Thank you anger for bringing your attention to me." Then ask, "Anger, what are you angry about?" Trust whatever you hear in your mind. You have set aside your ego and fears so you will hear the truth. Then ask, "Anger, what do you need in order to be healed?" Allow your anger to tell you what it needs in order to be healed. Again, anger will speak to you, and it may surprise you what it needs. You can then ask, "Anger, what else do you want to tell me or show me?" Be open to whatever you hear. You can repeat these questions. Once you feel complete with what you hear and need, thank anger for speaking to you. It is important to acknowledge your body and emotions for speaking to you.

❖ Here's another more detailed example using pain you discovered in your body:

Pain, thank you for getting my attention. Pain, what emotion is tied up around you? What do I need to know concerning the pain? Is there any person or situation that brings about this pain? If so, who or what? What do I need to know concerning the situation or person that brings about the pain? Body, what do you need from me in order to release the pain and be healed? Repeat the questions, and then ask the body if there is anything else it needs to tell you regarding the pain. Once you receive all of your information, thank your body's consciousness for speaking to you and for helping you to recognize and release the pain. When you have completed the process, notice how much the pain has diminished. In order for the pain to be released completely, you will have to do everything your body said it needed.

❖ Another method you can use on any type of pain is:

1. Gently close your eyes.

2. Take a slow deep breath in through your nose and exhale through your mouth.

3. Locate exactly where the pain is.

4. Give thanks for drawing your attention to it.

5. Look into the pain.

6. What color is it? Acknowledge the color you see.

7. What size is it? Acknowledge the size. Example— your fist, three inches, a dime.

8. What shape is the pain? Acknowledge it. Example—square, circle.

9. What texture do you see? Acknowledge it. Example—smooth, bumpy, rough.

10. What is the consistency? Acknowledge it. Example—liquid, thick like tar, gooey.

11. What is the depth of the pain? Acknowledge it. Example—six inches, two inches, one fourth inch.

12. Go back and repeat steps 5-11, and each time you do, the color, size, shape, texture, consistency, and depth of your pain will begin to change. Continue steps 5-11 three to five times. If after five times you still have the pain, ask yourself, "Do I want to release this pain?" If not, "Why?"

13. Take a deep breath in and exhale. When you feel comfortable open your eyes.

If you find it difficult to believe what you hear, or you aren't sure you hear anything, focus on the area in your body where you hold emotion. Then on a piece of paper write your questions, say them aloud, and without thinking write whatever comes to mind. Don't think about it. Just let your pen flow with the questions, and your answers will be revealed.

Now that you discovered where you are holding your emotions, and listened to or written down what your body needs to heal, you need to act on what you learned.

The first few times you do Body Dialogue you may think it is all in your head or mind, but the truth is if you listen, your body will speak to you—it always does. I encourage you to work with your emotions through Body Dialogue. This is a fun and easy way to discover the emotions stored in your body, release the negative ones, and embrace the positive ones.

æ∂   ∂§

Modalities to Move Energy in Your Body

When your body becomes stagnant or energy is blocked, discomfort, *dis-ease* and other problems can emerge. There are countless ways you can help the healing process when this happens. The following are some of the modalities I have found beneficial to my well-being and have used throughout the decades.

Remember, every person's body is different, so what works for one person may not work for another. Find what resonates with you. Also, use caution and consult with your medical professional.

❖ **Acupuncture** is a modality I have used consistently throughout my decades of healing. I started acupuncture in 1984 when I had anorexia. My treatments were to enhance my appetite, help with depression, increase my energy, and help me sleep. In 1987, I started having acupuncture treatments on a regular basis (2 to 4 times a month for HIV/AIDS symptoms) to build up my immune system, clear lung infections, regulate my constipation or severe diarrhea, strengthen my organs, release joint pain, keep me balanced and peaceful, and treat any other ailment I experienced.

Where I receive my acupuncture, I can choose between Chinese and Japanese treatments. It is amazing how quickly my body responds to Japanese acupuncture. It continues to be one of my main healing treatments. The purpose of acupuncture is to harmonize the internal energy (qi or chi, pronounced "chee"). This assists the body to heal and repair. Chi circulates in the body along 12 major energy pathways called meridians. Each meridian is linked to specific internal organs and organ systems. When hair-fine needles are inserted into specific acu-points just under the skin, the flow of energy is corrected and rebalanced, pain relieved, and health restored.

❖ **Alphabiotic Alignment** is a unique hands-on process which instantly unifies the brain hemispheres, balances energies within the nervous system and muscles, and facilitates the release of stress held within the mind/body. In this state of alignment you begin to function better on all levels—physical, mental, emotional, and spiritual—placing you in a more favorable position to heal yourself. I use Alphabiotic Alignment for my herniated disk and back pain. For more information, visit http://www.alphabiotics.net/Alignment.htm.

❖ **Bowen Therapy or Bowtech** was developed by Tom Bowen as holistic bodywork in Australia in the mid-1950s as a "gift from God." Bowen Therapy remains unique as a bodywork modality. This therapy moves over muscles or tendons, addressing the whole body, stimulating it to reset and heal itself. These gentle and powerful Bowen moves send impulses to the brain resulting in immediate muscle relaxation and pain reduction. The energetic healing may occur at any level as needed: physical, emotional, mental, or spiritual.

The difference between Bowen and other modalities involves the speed at which it works, how gentle it feels, and how long the pain relief lasts. Bowtech benefits everyone from newborns to the very elderly, trained athletes, and pregnant women. For more information, visit http://www.Bowtech.com.

❖ **Colorpuncture** is a system of holistic acu–light therapy in which different frequencies of visible light are applied onto the meridian where needles are typically place during acupuncture. By using various colors, energy can be manipulated, either to stimulate or sedate. Gentle, relaxing, and non-invasive, colorpuncture is sometimes used on people who are uncomfortable with needles.

❖ **CranioSacral Therapy** is a gentle, non-invasive, hands-on therapy that helps the body restore balance and harmony to the craniosacral system. Bodies are in constant motion externally and internally. Every joint, bone, muscle, vital organ, and soft tissue/membrane has its own unique rhythmic motion, and they are all synchronized within the craniosacral system.

CranioSacral Therapy has been shown to help with neck, shoulder, back pain, headaches, migraines, old injuries, whip-lash, TMJ, TMD, brain and spinal cord injuries, learning difficulties, ADD, ADHD, ear and eye problems, birth and delivery trauma, post-surgical recovery, and many other health challenges and conditions including emotional difficulties. For more information about CranioSacral Therapy visit these two websites: http://www.milneinstitute.com or http://www.upledger.com.

❖ **Energy Healing** is the multidimensional opening of the major energy centers (chakras) in the body to generate the vitality and life force energy needed for healing. This process works on many levels and uses guidance from higher states of consciousness. It enables you to live in your essence, free from old confining patterns. In some cases it allows you to become free of *dis-ease*. Energy healing can provide clearing, transformation, and awakening of the healing power within the chakra system.

Energy healing can also help establish a connection to your inner guides, and generate a greater sense of inner peace. It can facilitate the transformation of old patterns and allow you to live in your "juices" by being more connected to your essence. Energy healing can help you experience the core of who you are. With energy healing I experienced an increased vitality, a greater appreciation of life, and a release of sabotaging behaviors and blocked energy patterns.

❖ **Energy Medicine** — According to one of the pioneers of Energy Medicine, Donna Eden, "Energy Medicine is the body's natural medicine. Your body knows how to heal itself, and energy is its natural elixir. But we live in a world where the body's energies are pitted against one another and where we have lost touch with traditional wisdom for enhancing the body's self-healing abilities. Energy medicine teaches you how to maintain the body as a vibrant energy system and how to direct its energies for healing and health. In energy medicine, energy is the *medicine* (you heal the body by activating its natural healing energies), and energy is also the *patient* (you heal the body by restoring energies that have become weak, disturbed, or out of balance.) The methods are effective and surprisingly easy to learn. They can be used on a self-help basis, and they are very powerful when in the hands of a skilled health care practitioner." For more information, go to http://www.LearnEnergyMedicine.com.

❖ **Emotional Freedom Techniques and Related Energy Therapies (EFT).** Based on impressive recent discoveries and ancient healing practices involving the body's subtle energies, Emotional Freedom Techniques (EFT) and other energy therapies are proven clinically effective (over 80% of the time) for dramatically decreasing and/or eliminating a wide array of negative emotional states associated with trauma, stress, anxiety, fears, phobias, depression, grief, addictive cravings, and children's issues. Energy therapies have additionally provided relief from hundreds of physical symptoms including headaches, pain, and breathing difficulties. They can also be used to lessen learning disabilities, negative behaviors, and improve performance in talents, intellectual, and athletic endeavors.

These therapies often work where nothing else has by "tapping" into the body's energy, acupuncture (meridian), and cognitive systems to release negative trapped energy and blocks in the mind and body. Results are usually rapid, long lasting, and gentle. There are no drugs or equipment involved. EFT and related energy therapies are easily learned, fast, safe, and easy to assist others in using basic techniques. They can also be self-applied with the same amazing results. For more information, go to http://www.emofree.com.

❖ **Healing Touch (or Therapeutic Touch)** is a gentle, powerful, non-invasive healing modality. It is currently being used in many hospitals, health care centers, private practices, and homes as an adjunct to conventional methods of treatment. Healing Touch/ Therapeutic Touch has been known to alleviate pain, discomfort, and stress, and may promote and speed the healing process. It has been used with great success with infants born pre-

129

maturely and has had a profound effect on the terminally ill.

Healing Touch/Therapeutic Touch represents a conscious effort to draw upon universal energy, a subtle (non-physical) force that sustains all living organisms and directs flow for healing. The practitioner scans the client's energy field with their hands several inches from their client's skin, replenishing energy where necessary, releasing congestion, removing obstructions, and restoring order and balance.

❖ **Homeopathy** is a unique system of health care based on the principle that all illness starts as an energetic imbalance which expresses itself as symptoms, sensations, and feelings in body, mind, and emotions. For example, one may get migraine headaches, have allergies, and be nervous and restless. The way this combination of symptoms is experienced and how the person reacts will be unique. Understanding the person and all the symptoms as a unified whole leads to the selection of a single homeopathic remedy that heals the headache, the allergies, and the nervousness and restlessness. Most of all, it heals the underlying cause, the energetic imbalance, leading to lasting improvement.

Homeopathic treatment is based on the natural principle that like cures like, or in other words, the symptoms that a medicine can cause in a healthy person are the symptoms it can cure. Another universal law states that for every action there is an equal and opposite reaction. The homeopathic remedy is a match to the disturbing energy and causes a vital reaction within the person to oppose the symptoms. Healing begins the same way anti-venom helps heal the symptoms of a poisonous snakebite. For

more information, visit
http://nationalcenterforhomeopathy.org.

❖ **Hypnotherapy** has proven beneficial to lots of people dealing with addictions, weight issues, pain, health problems, anxiety, fears, depression, and to improve self-image. Hypnotherapy has been useful for me when I found it difficult to eat due to anorexia, or when dealing with chronic emotional issues.

❖ **Kalos Transformational Healing** is a gentle way of penetrating the sub-conscious mind and effectively turning on the immune system. Healing is a result of our body, mind, and emotions working in harmony with each other. The techniques have proven to be powerfully effective, striking at the heart of the physical, spiritual, or emotional problem.

Every problem has a cause. Through the Kalos methods, the cause can be easily identified and addressed through The Ten Priority System, which includes balancing the body's nutritional support, adding necessary vitamins and minerals, identifying food allergies, detoxification, body structure, electrical system, endocrine system, organs, emotional stress, exercise, and proper rest. You can uncover the root cause of your problem and resolve it! For more information, visit http://www.kalos.org.

❖ **The L.A.M.P. Process – Listening to Applied Modern Physicists.** Toward the end of the 20th century, quantum physicists proved the existence of a ubiquitous field that has been referred to for centuries. This field is the source and sustainer of all that is in the physical world of time and space. They call it the "Zero Point Field" (ZPF). It has been called by many other names including Holy

Spirit, Shekena, Grace, The Force, Christ Consciousness, etc. Like prayer, it responds to requests, however, like sunshine and rain it is for everyone's use. It responds to each individual's conscious intention. However, that intention is modified by one's core beliefs. It is the source of disease and healing, of good luck and bad, of the experiences you encounter in your day-to-day life and the outcomes of how you deal with them. It generates all that comprises the physical world and your mental and emotional worlds. The journey is designed as an easy way to involve the ZPF in shifting you into a more optimal life and body. It doesn't involve psychiatry, psychology, or hypnosis. For more information call 1-800-711-5903, Infinite Possibilities Productions.

❖ **Massage** provides a peaceful, relaxed environment to let go of stress and tension. It can aid the body's circulation of blood and lymph to promote health and healing. There are various forms of massage from very light to deep tissue. My body responds well to Tai massage, Tuina, Shiatsu, and Lomilomi (traditional Hawaiian massage). I treat my body to at least one massage a month.

❖ **Music Therapy** is based on the idea that bodies are energy, and blockages can be moved with music or sound. Music therapy has been used for almost 50 years in the treatment and rehabilitation of people with AIDS, cancer, stroke, substance abuse, and pain.

From time to time, I attend a Drum Circle with a group of vibrant women, and I find the rhythm and the vibration of the Native traditional instruments, such as the drums, Tibetan bells, crystal bowls, chimes, rattles, and other instruments extremely healing. I also listen to specific music to enhance the wellness of my mind-body-spirit.

❖ **Osteopathic Medicine** is a system of comprehensive medical care that goes beyond conventional medical philosophy to include an emphasis on structural balance of the musculo-skeletal system. One of my main doctors in San Diego is Melissa Noble, D.O. She is a specialist in Osteopathic Medicine. Osteopathic physicians use joint manipulation, postural re-education, and physical therapy to normalize the body's structure and promote healing. Most medical conditions are amenable to osteopathic healing. In some cases, osteopathy has been shown to resolve illnesses resistant to surgery and other medical approaches. For more information, visit http://www.osteopathic.org.

❖ **Qigong** (pronounced "chi kung") is a combination of two ideas: "qi" meaning air, breath of life, or vital energy of the body, and "gong" meaning the skill of working with, or cultivating, self-discipline and achievement. The art of Qigong consists primarily of meditation, relaxation, physical movement, mind-body integration, and breathing exercises to balance and strengthen the body's vital energy. When I developed an awareness of qi sensations (energy) in my body, I could use my mind to guide the qi to the different organs in my body for healing.

❖ **Rebirthing** is a breathing process that increases our ability to feel and resolve the effects of our past. It involves breathing in a full, free manner (as guided by a trained Rebirther); the result is an increase in the level of physical and spiritual energy in our body, thus cleansing the many tensions held there. The result of the physical cleansing is that the mental and emotional origins of tension come back into consciousness and can then be healed. By learning to breathe consciously and fully, we discover and release the core issues now held in our mind and emotions.

Rebirthing can be in group settings, or with an individual. Every session with a Rebirther involves both counseling and the breathing process. Rebirthing leaves you with an incredible sense of peace, aliveness, and true self-worth.

Leonard Orr, founder of the Rebirthing philosophy, states, "Rebirthing breath causes the inner breath to be connected to the outer breath. Inner breath can also be called pure life, spirit, God, or infinite being. The outer breath is air, oxygen, and the respiratory system."

❖ **Reflexology** is the technique of applying pressure with thumbs and fingers to specific areas of the feet. Its origin can be traced to the Ancient Egyptians, but the form of reflexology didn't come together until the 1930s. Reflexologists contend that the body and all of its organs and glands are mapped on either the foot or the hand.

Reflexology can be used to heal the body with only touching the extremities—hands and feet. Reflexology can help issues such as headache, low back pain, insomnia, menstrual cramps, constipation, as well as providing overall relaxation and preventative maintenance.

❖ **Reiki** is an ancient science of energy. The use of Reiki is the simple transition of Reiki energy from one person to another through touch. The practitioner has been trained to use the energy along with symbols.

❖ **Tai Chi** is a Chinese healing art using a series of gentle flowing physical exercises for mind and body. Chi or vital life energy is moved throughout the meridian pathways of the body. By increasing stamina, flexibility, relaxation and overall quality of life, the healing process is encouraged and accelerated.

❖ **Yoga** means union or integration of physical, mental, and spiritual energies to enhance health and well-being. It is a complete science of life that originated in India thousands of years ago. The physical postures, breathing exercises, and meditation practices of yoga reduce stress, lower blood pressure, and regulate heart rate. There are various forms of yoga, each unique.

If your body is in a weakened state and you aren't able to do any of the above modalities, there's still something you can do. I remember when I was so sick I could hardly get out of bed, let alone leave the house. When I was homebound, I would have a friend or loved one lay me on my back on the floor and place the bottoms of my feet on a small trampoline. Then I would have them jump on the trampoline. As they jumped, I could feel the vibration and movement go into my body. I believe this allowed my body to move energy and help with my circulation and healing process.

One of the natural ways to cleanse and balance your body is to walk barefoot on grass, or close to a tree. Your body responds to these stimulants as it detoxifies itself from all the electrical currents you have accumulated throughout the day and night. Make this a daily 5 to 15 minute practice, and reap the benefits.

Everybody is different, so what works for one person may not work for another. Be open to possibilities and discover what modalities resonate with you.

Vibrational Healing Products

If we are primarily energy, why not use different modalities to help restore, move, balance, and clear blocked energy? I believe Vibrational Healing will be the healing of the future.

I have used a couple of outstanding energy vibration products which I have found extremely helpful in my healing such as:

❖ Pulsors—Electromagnetic Pollution is everyone's problem. In our modern world, we are constantly bombarded by unseen energy fields that sap our vitality, leaving us tense, frustrated, and tired, and they have a profound effect on our mental and physical health. These fields are created by each electrical device around us. Research is proving that electromagnetic radiation decreases our melatonin levels, and recent news reports reveal cellular phones may be a contributing factor in the development of brain tumors, among other illnesses. It is estimated today we experience 200 million times more electromagnetic radiation than in pre-industrial times. We are just not capable of nor designed to handle this overwhelming irritation and interference!

This is a critical problem because the natural human energy field becomes distorted when under the effect of these inescapable, artificial energy fields. This energetic distortion can lead to various behavioral, psychological, and even gross physiological disturbances. This distortion happens because our energy fields function on the principle of resonance, and these external fields alter our natural vibratory patterns and rates, much like the static distortion of a pure radio signal. We can try to mitigate these negative effects by avoiding contact with or increasing distance from electrical devices, but we cannot avoid the fields generated by household wiring, transmission lines, or those due to information trans-missions, such as cell towers.

Devices are available which can change the basic nature of these dis-coordinating fields so they no longer interfere with our natural energy field. These devices are called Pulsor Polarity Protectors. Also, there are Pulsor tools which can be used therapeutically to remove the effects caused by these distortions in the energy field, offering an easy, lasting method for energy balancing and deeper states of relaxation. Through the use of these devices, which can be worn as a decorative pendant, placed in a pocket, or used in the environment, your personal energy field can be protected from the distortions caused by the myriad external energy fields that constantly surround us. This allows you to experience greater focus and calm and even increased energy, since one no longer needs to struggle as much to keep one's energetic center.

I use pulsors and highly recommend every person and household use them. For further information, visit http://www.energyintegrity.com.

I have also used sound, light, and crystal therapy at different times in my healing process. Each has its own unique vibration and each is capable of tuning and balancing the body.

❖ Sound—Sound affects our state of mind, and different vibrations correlate to body parts. I have experienced healings through the use of music, crystal bowls, singing bowls, Tibetan bowls, various kinds of tuning forks, drumming, chanting, singing, and toning.

The vibration of sound is healing as it moves the energy in the body and resonates with the soul and spirit. An amazing friend of mine, Monica, owns a set of seven crystal singing bowls of various sizes according to the chakras. When I lie on the floor and she plays the bowls, the harmonious, magical sound vibrates throughout my body and surroundings. The sound can lift my energy, calm me, or take me to other dimensions.

The company Monica purchased her crystal singing bowls from, Crystal Tones, has reasonable prices, and the bowls have the highest quality of sound I have heard. "Alchemy" bowls is the name for all the specialized quartz crystal bowls embedded with minerals such as moldavite, cyanite, gold, rose quartz, etc. These are almost always lightweight, clear, or opaque bowls. The company also has a series of bowls of all colors called the "Therapeutic Series". All bowls are therapeutic from a vibrational energy perspective. For more information, call 800-358-9492 or go to http://www.crystalsingingbowls.com.

❖ Light—Like sound, different colors also carry different frequencies. I have experienced Light Therapy from time to time with a professional practitioner. As I lie on a comfortable massage table, a spectrum of colors are focused on areas of my body. The colors and areas of the body depend on what I am experiencing at the time. For example, for my blood and circulation, a red light will shine on my body. Lavender light may be used for relaxation or calming. For my lung problems, I have had a green and sometimes blue light shining directly on my lungs. The various spectrums of light are used not only for physical problems, but also emotional healing.

Today you will find many applications of light therapy in doctors' offices worldwide: infrared for pain relief, ultraviolet in surgery rooms to prevent bacterial infections, or blue light treatment for faster healing in post-op care.

❖ Crystals—Crystals can be used as a healing tool, which I have found to be beneficial for years. Each crystal has its own vibration, purpose, and use. I only work with crystals to which I am drawn. If you become aware of a crystal's consciousness, you will discover how it wants to be used, for what purposes, and what it has to teach you. This is outlined in The Spirit Chapter, sub-chapter "Communicating with the Kingdoms."

There are numerous kinds of crystals, but the main ones I work with are:

❖ Smoky Quartz—helps with emotional security, releases negativity, grounding, and protection. Smoky Quartz is associated with the root chakra.

❖ Carnelian—helps with your self-image, vitality, motivation, and personal power. Carnelian can be used on the spleen/sacral chakra.

❖ Chrysocolla—promotes inner strength, draws off negativity. This is a good crystal for the solar plexus.

❖ Rose Quartz—promotes unconditional love, peace, heals the heart, forgiveness, and brings a sense of calmness. This crystal is associated with the heart chakra.

❖ Lapis Lazuli—assists in speaking your truth, expands awareness, and self-expression. I have used this crystal on my throat chakra and to open the third eye.

❖ Sodalite—helps with understanding, confidence, truth, intuition, and spiritual perception. This crystal is good for the third eye chakra.

❖ Amethyst—strengthens your intuition, clarity, higher states of consciousness, tranquility, and Divine Love. The amethyst is associated with the crown chakra.

❖ Quartz—amplifies the power of other crystals, and is great for meditation. Quartz can be used on any part of your body.

❖ Tourmaline—comes in different colors and is used to boost confidence, understand yourself and others, and grounds spiritual energy.

❖ Hematite—is excellent for grounding, magnetizing, and energizing.

❖ Malachite—powerful balancing stone for all of the bodies.

It is important to mention again there are a lot more crystals than what I have mentioned. Each can be used in a different way, and have a lot of different healing properties. Once you become in tune to your body and the consciousness of crystals, you will know how to use them for your highest good.

Just because a crystal is large doesn't make it more powerful. Some of my strongest crystals are small and delicate. Feel the energy from the crystals you are drawn to, and know it is the perfect one for you.

After you are drawn to certain crystals, turn them in all different directions and notice what you see inside, through the sides, on the top looking down, and on the bottom looking up. Perhaps you will see rainbows, stars, figures, angels, mountains, birds, or the money symbol. Stories are held within the crystals. Enjoy listening to them.

When you purchase any crystal, it is important to cleanse it to release the vibration and energy of other people who have held it or used it in some way. Below are various ways I have cleansed my crystals:

1. Place them in sea salts and water for a minimum of seven hours. Fill the bowl with spring water to cover the crystals one inch over the top. For more refined energies, use distilled water. For each crystal, add one tablespoon of sea salt to spring water. You can also cover your crystals with the dry sea salt and place them out in the sun. Please note salt or water may damage some crystals, so when you purchase them, ask which is the best way for you to cleanse your new crystals.

2. You can smudge (fan smoke) over your crystals with sage, sweet grass, incense, or frankincense. This is great for crystals that cannot be soaked in salt water. Use a feather fan for smudging and not your hand. Passing your hand in the negative energies (smoke) you are releasing from the crystal may attract them to you, so smudge yourself after you have cleansed your crystals.

3. The moonlight is a powerful way to charge and cleanse crystals. Place them outside under a full moon to charge them and a new moon to cleanse your crystals.

4. You can bury your crystals in Mother Earth for cleansing. When I have used a crystal for healings and a lot of negativity has been released, I usually place my crystals in the soil. I dig a hole in Mother Earth or in a flower pot larger than the crystal. Then I place my crystal point down and cover it with soil. When I bury my crystals outside, I mark the area and uncover it the next day or later, depending on the energy.

5. A simple way to cleanse crystals is with your sacred breath. Hold it between your fingers and blow away the negativity. As you blow, ask your Higher Self to cleanse your crystal.

6. After using my crystals for healings, sometimes I will clear them by running cold tap water over them, with the point down. The reason for having the point down is so the negative energy is washed down the drain. It is important never to use warm or hot water because it can fracture or break your crystal.

Each crystal has its own vibration, and you can program your crystals on something specifically, or ask the crystal what it wants.

Hold the crystal in your hand and sense its energy. Then visualize or sense how you would like to use the crystal. Next ask the crystal if it is willing to be used in the way you desire. If the crystal agrees, you may notice it becomes warmer or you might feel a strong tingling sensation in your hands.

You can also go to The Spirit Chapter, sub-chapter "Communicating with the Kingdoms" and listen to the crystal's answers. Once you hear your answers, thank the crystal.

If you have been drawn to a crystal there is a reason. I know when I am immediately attracted to one it is for my highest good. Then I will ask the crystal how it wants to be used and what it wants to teach or show me. I then give thanks to the crystal and look forward to using it the way it would like to be used.

Enjoy the beauty, vibration, energy, and healing abilities of the crystals to which you are drawn. If you have an assortment of crystals before you, close your eyes and move your hand slowly over the crystals and notice what one(s) sends out warmth, tingling, movement, or energy. Or perhaps your hand will stop on top of certain crystals. Know those are the perfect crystals for you.

The Use of Energy

In this chapter, sub-chapter entitled, "Modalities to Move Energy in Your Body," I shared various modalities that worked for me. I would also like to emphasize another way to move energy in your body.

❖ Here are a few exercises I teach people to get in touch with energy, and how to use it:

1. Place your hands vertically in front of you, thumbs up, about a foot apart, holding them at whatever level feels comfortable.

2. Bend your fingers inward as if they were grabbing onto a ball with palms facing. Begin to rotate both hands in different directions, back and forth, clockwise then counter clockwise, but not in the same direction.

3. As you rotate your cupped fingers, slowly begin to notice the movement and energy in the area between your hands.

4. Now increase the speed a little.

5. Then move your hands apart (fingers still close together in a cupped position) as if you are playing an accordion. Move your hands in and out. Feel the tension, the energy. See how far you can move your hands apart and still feel the energy. Keep moving

them back and forth like an accordion until you feel a lot of energy.

6. You may want to repeat these steps after 10 or so seconds to create a stronger intense energy.

7. Once you feel the energy build up, you can harness it by placing your hands on an area of your body that needs healing, releasing, or relaxation. Just lay your hands flat on that area. You may feel warmth or a tingling sensation.

❖ With a friend or loved one you can do the following:

1. Have them do the same exercise as above, along with you, but at step 5 have your friend or loved one stand about two feet in front of you and place their hands vertically across from yours, (hands straight up) so your hands are lined up with one another.

2. Now become each other's accordion, moving the hands forward and backward.

3. Feel the energy between you.

4. Move apart another foot or so, and see if you can still feel the energy between you as you move your hands back and forth.

5. Continue to move apart another foot at a time. Then stop and feel the energy.

6. See how far you can move away from each other until you can no longer feel the connection or energy.

❖ Now that you have become aware of what the energy feels like, you can also do the following with your friend or loved one:

1. Stand face to face about a foot-and-a-half away from each other.

2. Focus your attention on your heart chakra (center of your chest) and feel the energy in that area.

3. You may want to close your eyes to really feel it.

4. Once you feel the energy in your heart chakra, become aware of the energy in your friend or loved one's heart center.

5. After the two of you become aware of each other's energy, move away from each other a foot at a time (both at the same time).

6. With each step, notice the energy between you.

7. Continue to move apart from one another until you no longer feel the other person's energy.

8. If you had your eyes closed, now open them and notice the distance between you.

❖ When I go into a crowded area, movie theater, doctor's office, hospital, restaurant, airport, or somewhere I might pick up negative feelings or energy, I have found it beneficial to envision a brilliant white light cocoon around my body. The white light surrounds me above my head, around my entire body, and below my feet. Doing this visualization helps me to keep my energy level up, and I don't feel drained or tired.

You can also consciously send out loving energy to people you come in contact with, and you will remain strong.

Enjoy keeping your energy up and vibrant—feeling energized and alive.

Exercise, Exercise, Exercise

Exercise is extremely important to your well-being. Find an exercise you enjoy doing and would look forward to participating in regularly such as swimming, jogging, brisk walks, yoga, bicycling, or sports.

You can make exercise fun by listening to music, having your friend join you, visualizing images, using affirmations or incantations, and charting your progress.

Here are some of the benefits of regular exercise:

1. Reduces heart disease.
2. Improves your well-being.
3. Lowers high blood pressure.
4. Decreases the development of diabetes.
5. Builds and maintains healthy muscles, joints, and bones.

Aerobic exercise can assist in some of the following ways:

1. Reduces body fat.
2. Increases oxygen.
3. Assists weight control.
4. Enhances cardiovascular system (heart and lungs).
5. Improves glucose tolerance and reduces insulin resistance.

Strength or weight exercises also have benefits, such as:

1. Reduces body fat.

2. Strengthens muscles.
3. Lowers cholesterol.
4. Increases flexibility.
5. Increases lean body mass.

To improve your balance and coordination you may want to take up dancing, Tai Chi, skiing, bowls/boules, or yoga.

Exercises to promote flexibility are yoga, Pilates, and Tai Chi.

Some weight-bearing exercises to prevent osteoporosis would include walking, dancing, rebounding on a mini-trampoline, stair climbing, golf, and racquet sports.

Several exercises to improve your energy and activate qi are breathing exercises, Qigong, swimming in cold water, the Five Rites of Rejuvenation, and Chinese balls.

I find when I schedule my exercise program every week on the same days and times, seldom will I allow other activities to interfere. Exercise is a vital part of my wellness.

If you or anyone you know is unable to get out of the house to exercise, I have included an exercise in this chapter, sub-chapter "Modalities to Move Energy in Your Body." It is located at the end of the section.

Look Into the Mirror

Look into the mirror. What kinds of feelings come up for you? Do you feel liberated, or do you feel like hiding? What sensations do you feel in your body? What is your response? Some familiar thoughts or sayings might be:

- ❖ I am fat.
- ❖ I am ugly.
- ❖ I hate you.
- ❖ I am boney.
- ❖ I am so old.
- ❖ I hate my hair.
- ❖ I hate my scar.
- ❖ I hate my breasts.
- ❖ Any many more. . . .

Or maybe you walk right past a mirror and won't even look into it—especially if it is a full-length mirror. When was the last time you really looked at yourself?

When I was challenged with self-esteem and self-image issues, Linda had me look into the mirror each morning, stare deep into my eyes, and express from the center of my heart, "I love you. I really love you." At first, it seemed weird and hard to do. However, before long it felt comfortable.

Then as I looked into the mirror, I fixed my eyes on different parts of my face and upper body and told each part I loved it just the way it was. It took a while to have a sincere smile when I spoke to my body. A few months later, I was able to stand nude in front of a full-length mirror and look at my entire body, front, back, and both sides and say, "I love you. I really love you, just the way you are."

Our society is so caught up in glamour and looking perfect, we have forgotten we are perfect just the way we are. True beauty lies within each person. Every person is unique in his or her own way. Physically, if you want to lose or gain weight, then do something about it. However, don't compare yourself to the models in the magazines. Love yourself and your body. The more you do, the quicker it will be the body you love.

We truly are blessed with each part of our body, so why not give gratitude for all it has done for us?

- ❖ Your eyes see beauty.
- ❖ Your ears hear loving words.
- ❖ Your nose smells fragrances.
- ❖ Your mouth and voice for speaking.
- ❖ Your legs and feet allow you to walk.
- ❖ Your hands embrace and grasp objects.

What about your organs that maybe you have taken for granted:

- ❖ Your lungs breathe in oxygen.
- ❖ Your heart is your life force.
- ❖ Your muscles helping you move.
- ❖ Your stomach digests your food.

I remember back in the mid-1980s, I would stand in front of the mirror and sing different songs to imprint who I was. My two favorite songs were Jerry Florence and Alliance's "I Love Myself the Way I Am" and Whitney Houston's "A Hero Lies Within."

Jerry was a singer, songwriter, and record producer. In the mid-80s, he formed Jerry Florence and Alliance, which was a three-person vocal group. Jerry was a talented, gifted man who loved life, and his music was an expression of a world in unity and peace. A lot of New Thought church members sing his songs.

Jerry and I were active in the AIDS community at the same time. Unfortunately in 1994, he died from AIDS complications. Our community grieved his death. However, Jerry and his music will forever live in my heart.

You can purchase Jerry Florence and Alliance music on the Internet at,
http://www.heartinspired.com/audio/jerryflorence.htm.

If it takes music for you to feel comfortable standing in front of a mirror and looking at yourself, engage in music, any type of music, and begin to love your entire self more deeply. There are many uplifting and inspirational songs today to boost your self-esteem, self-image, and your perspective on life. Listen to the words and embrace the songs to which you are drawn. They can excite you and help you feel good about yourself.

When you look into the mirror and practice these steps, you can make great changes in a short amount of time. See your Divine Being!

ے۔ ؎

Sexually Transmitted Diseases

Our bodies are sacred, yet many men, women, young adults, and children treat their bodies as if they are toys, then play with no consideration of consequences.

There are various types of Sexually Transmitted Diseases (STDs) such as, but not limited to:

- ❖ Gonorrhea
- ❖ Chlamydia and LGV
- ❖ Syphilis
- ❖ Genital Herpes
- ❖ Hepatitis B
- ❖ Human Immunodeficiency Virus (HIV)
- ❖ Human Papillomavirus (HPV)
- ❖ Pelvic Inflammatory Disease (PID)
- ❖ Non-specific Urethritis
- ❖ Bacterial Vaginosis
- ❖ Chancroid
- ❖ Trichomoniasis
- ❖ Cytomegalovirus

Every one of these diseases is preventable, but only when every person takes responsibility for his or her life, well-being, actions, and behaviors.

In 1983, I married Bill. He was mentally and emotionally abusive toward me. However, nothing shocked me as much as when I discovered he was infected with AIDS.

In 1986, after being divorced from Bill for several years, I saw him on Dan Rather's AIDS special entitled AIDS Hits Home, announcing to the world he was infected with AIDS. I immediately called Bill, and he denied it was him. However, during my meditation, I was told Bill was infected and he infected me. My tests came back positive. Thank God I didn't infect my soon-to-be-husband, Sid.

In many ways I felt blessed because I was already working in the AIDS Community and I understood the virus and the problems associated with the *dis-ease* and being infected.

Bill called me a few years later, days before he died from AIDS complications, and admitted it was him on Dan Rather's AIDS special. Then he went on to tell me he knew he was infected when he married me but didn't know how to tell me. During the time Bill became infected it wasn't called AIDS, but GRID – *Gay Related Immune Disease*. Bill lived a secret bisexual life of which I was unaware, and he believed he couldn't infect me.

There are several reasons I share this with you:

❖ Unfortunately, there are many married and unmarried men and women in relationships that aren't monogamous. The unfaithful person may be so good at hiding their secret that the partner has no idea what is going on. Who knows if the unfaithful partner is using protection when sexually active?

❖ It is extremely important for you to realize no one knows if they are infected with HIV/AIDS until they become sick or get tested.

❖ You may think you know your partner, but when you have sex with one person, you aren't only taking them to bed with you, you are also taking all of the previous partners and their partners, all the way back in time.

❖ You may say they dress well, are well educated, live in a nice neighborhood, and look healthy so you don't have to be concerned. That is a false belief.

❖ HIV/AIDS doesn't discriminate, but people do, and that is wrong! I have been infected since 1983, and people still discriminate against infected men, women, and children. Unfortunately, for some people they won't understand and show compassion until a friend or loved one becomes infected.

❖ In 1987, I went public with my story nationally and internationally to educate people about the myths and reality of HIV/AIDS, other sexually transmitted diseases, and alternative therapies. People wanted to treat me as an innocent victim because I was a woman and became infected by my husband. My message has always been and will continue be "Every man, woman, and child deserves the same respect, compassion, love, and understanding, regardless of how they became infected. I shouldn't be treated any differently than any other person infected with HIV or AIDS."

❖ Proper education is important, because all sexually transmitted diseases are preventable. Some people don't believe in STD education, but once a friend or family member becomes infected, it is too late.

❖ Take responsibility for all of your behaviors, especially if you have been drinking or using any kind of substance that could impair your judgment.

❖ There are a lot of consequences to being infected with a sexually transmitted disease. You face the reality of anything from impotence to death!

❖ WAKE UP!!! This could happen to you. This could happen to your children, your brothers and sisters, your best friend, or your parents and grandparents. Don't take life for granted.

❖ The only people safe from sexually transmitted diseases are those men, women, and children who abstain.

❖ Take responsibility for your life and well-being. Love your body and self enough to say NO to unprotected sex.

I remember after I dated a man for six months, our relationship grew stronger, and one night he wanted to make love. I was open to it because I really had strong feelings for him. However, I wasn't going to make love unless he used a condom. (Female condoms weren't available yet). Russell knew I was infected, yet he insisted he wouldn't use one. What does that tell you about Russell? When I share this story with college students, these are some of the responses I receive:

1. Maybe he was already infected with HIV/AIDS but didn't tell me. My answer is, we still would have to protect ourselves, because there are different strains of the virus.

2. Maybe he loved me so much he didn't care. My answer is, I wouldn't call that love.

3. Maybe he was in denial thinking it couldn't happen to him. My answer is, yes, most people are in denial

156

thinking it cannot happen to them, but does that mean have unprotected sex? NO!

4. Maybe he felt a few seconds of pleasure was more important to him then his life. HMMM! That statement made the students think.

5. The reality is if Russell was willing to have unprotected sex with me, he probably had unprotected sex with his previous partners. Russell knew I was infected. I was honest with him. However, there are a lot of men and women who are infected that aren't honest with their partners. If I would have had a female condom, I could have used it. My refusal to make love with Russell that night caused our relationship to end.

I know some men and women don't believe they can find someone to love them because they are infected with HIV/AIDS or other sexually transmitted diseases. It is important to remember being infected isn't who you are; it is a *dis-ease*. Being infected doesn't make you any less of a person. In fact, you may become a stronger person. You need to be honest with men and women with whom you have intimate relationships.

Take responsibility for your well-being and life!

᠀   ᠀

Don't Make Your Doctor God

In 1987, I had only three t–cells, and my doctor told me if I didn't take a new drug called AZT (an HIV/AIDS medication) I would die within six months. The next morning I did muscle testing to see if AZT would be good for me. My body said No! Then during my prayers and meditation, I asked if it was for my highest good to take the AZT, and I was told it wasn't for my highest good to take it. Receiving a message from my body and from my meditation, I knew in my heart I had to refuse the new drug. I called my doctor, rejected the pills, and accepted his death sentence. I got all of my affairs in order: my will, durable power of attorney, and advance health care directive. I asked my parents if they would raise my loving daughter Jeaneen (then 12) when I died.

After my affairs were in order, one morning I sat in meditation and heard, *"My Child, why have you made your doctor God? Why have you bought into his death sentence? He does not know how or when you are going to die."*

Hearing those words was an immediate "wake up" call for me. I began to search for a new doctor using the following guidelines:

1. I prepare interview questions for the doctor.

2. I determine if they believe in or respect the methods of healing I value, such as traditional, Western, alternative, or Integrative Medicine.

3. The doctor must be as knowledgeable as I am about my illness.

4. During my appointment, I require they give me all the time I need to ask questions and go over details.

5. I need to feel comfortable and respected by the doctor.

6. If I decide to have a second option, the doctor would respect it.

7. The doctor must return my phone calls in a reasonable amount of time.

8. I make sure the doctor has medical rights in the hospital I prefer.

9. If I were hospitalized, I need to feel confident the doctor would have good bedside manners.

Don't be ashamed to look for another doctor if your needs aren't being met. Take your health and well-being into your own hands, and find a doctor or health professional with whom you can partner.

After I found my holistic doctor, Joan Priestley, I named my three t–cells Hope, Love, and Laughter and gave them the power and permission to assist me to heal.

ॐ   ॐ

A Weakened Body

No matter how healthy you are, there may be a time your body becomes weakened or *dis-eased* and requires admission into a hospital. I have spent many, many months in hospitals due to AIDS complications and I have learned a lot from my experiences that I would like to share.

❖ No matter how healthy or "*dis-eased*" you feel, no one knows when their last breath will be. Before being admitted into the hospital (if you know in advance) have your legal affairs in order. At least have your Living Will, also known as a Power of Attorney for Health Care or Advance Healthcare Directive. You can appoint someone as your proxy or representative to make decisions on maintaining extraordinary life-support if you become too ill, are in a coma, or are certain to die. You can also state certain people whom you do or do not want to visit you.

❖ As you are admitted to your hospital room, use alcohol pads to clean off things such as the telephone, handrails, nurse's call button, and television control. If you are unable to do this, ask your friend or loved one to do it for you. I know the hospital staff cleans the rooms extensively, but this is an additional precaution.

You can also combine 2-3 drops of pure lemon essential oils with water in a spray bottle to help cleanse and sanitize surfaces.

❖ Have advocates work for you with the doctors and nurses. Give them the authority to look at your chart, ask questions and obtain knowledge about your procedures and medications.

❖ Ask several close friends or loved ones to stop by to check on you regularly. They can bring you things from home or the store. Have them arrange your room to make you feel more comfortable. Perhaps you would like to have them set up your favorite photos, a plant, or other items meaningful to you that would make you feel more comfortable in your hospital room.

❖ They can help you bathe, eat, brush your hair, and if you are able, take you on walks. They can refill your water and get you a snack. Let your friends and loved ones be there for you in whatever way *you* desire.

❖ The night before or day of an operation or any kind of invasive procedures, I recommend you think of all the negative feelings, circumstances, and emotions you haven't expressed, or are still holding you back. Really focus on all the negativity that no longer serves you. As you think about the people, circumstances, and feelings, place them in the area where you know you will be operated on. Visualize all the negativity in that one particular area. Right before you go in for your operation or procedures know in your heart all negative feelings will be removed during your operation.

After your procedure, when you feel comfortable, visualize and fill the area that was operated on with love, joy, excitement, peace, and healing energy.

❖ If you are going to have an operation or any kind of procedure, it is important and helpful to have someone close to you be your "support" as you go into the procedure and come out of the recovery room.

❖ Mark the area you will be operated on (in pen), before going into the operating room.

❖ Question....always, always, always, question what is being given to you or going to be done to you. It doesn't matter if you think you know. Question it to make sure you are given the right medication and the right dosage. If you are offered something you aren't sure you are supposed to be taking, refuse it until you can talk to your doctor or your advocate. Unfortunately, hospital staff can mix up medications because of workload and time pressures.

When I was in the hospital receiving IV treatments, a nurse came in and said I needed another dose of my medication. I questioned her at least five times, stating I had just had IV treatments about an hour before. She insisted I was wrong. I was kind of groggy, but still believed I had received the medication. After questioning the nurse again, I gave up on my intuition and memory and let her hook me up to the IV.

Within an hour, my entire neurological system began to shut down. It was hard to talk; I couldn't remember things as simple as numbers and names, and it was difficult to move. The neurological doctor told me that due to an overdose of medication, my problems may or may not be permanent. Fortunately, after a day and a half, my neurological system returned to normal.

❖ Trust your instincts and have a friend or family member as your advocate. Be responsible for your well-being while in the hospital. Don't come out worse than you went in.

❖ Hospital Visitations—When I was in the hospital, at times I was so weak I couldn't do anything for myself: walk, sit up, move, go to the bathroom. Many times, visitors would come to see me. It took every ounce of energy I had just to say a few sentences. Yet, some people who visited carried on conversations about nothing of importance. My therapist, Penelope Eicher, saw what was happening and placed a notice on my door that read:

If you want to help Sharon please:

Limit your visit to no more than 10 minutes.
Sit quietly.
Read to her.
Ask her if she needs anything.
Softly play her favorite music.
Gently massage her feet, legs, or hands.
Talk only about what is important, from your heart.

Here are a few more suggestions for visitors:

1. When you visit a sick person, check your emotional baggage at the door. A sick person doesn't have the strength to hear about your problems.

2. Don't minimize the sick or dying person's feelings.

3. Don't assume their desire is to recover or not recover. Allow whatever feelings are being expressed.

4. Express your love, friendship, and respect for the person. There is magic in the telling and hearing.

5. SIT DOWN! Be nearer to eye level of the person in bed. Sit near the head of the bed and hold hands, if comfortable.

6. Be willing to listen, even to the silence.

7. Say prayers.

8. Hug the sick or dying person, if they are physically up for it. Ask first.

If you need a sign placed outside your door, then make that known. You don't want or need to have extra stress in your life when your body is in the healing process.

I understand family members and loved ones want to stay longer, and that is fine, if you are up to it. But other people need to realize how much energy it takes to have visitors talk and talk and talk about nothing of importance. They may feel uncomfortable, so they chatter.

Listen to your heart. You have permission not be social while in the hospital. Select the people who visit you and say no to the others. If you are too weak to tell people not to visit, have your advocates carry out your wishes. While in the hospital, if you want, you can ask people to send cards or flowers. You can read the cards over and over, if you choose, and place them in an area that will cheer you up when you look at them. Cards remind you to feel the support and love of your friends through the words and well wishes.

❖ No one knows when they are going to die. If you don't know how to start up a conversation with someone who is dying or if they are in denial about the seriousness of their illness, a question you can ask is, "If you were to die today, what would you want to tell me?" Then listen to what they have to say. Take time to tell them what you would want to say.

I suggested a friend of mine do this with her father, and at first they screamed at each other, blamed one another for various things, and anger came out of them like a volcano. However, once they realized for 40 some years they had misjudged one another on something that was misunderstood, they cried, held each other, kissed, and planned a trip together. Those simple words, "If you were to die today, what would you want to tell me?" can heal a relationship, bring closure, love, and inner peace. What a gift to receive and give before the person dies.

❖ At what point does a person decide the quality of life is more important than the quantity? When my life deteriorated, I no longer wanted to prolong my life. Not only was I suffering, but so were my daughter and the rest of my family.

Many times loved ones are so connected to the person who is dying they cling onto them and don't allow the person to make their transition. Give your friend or loved one permission to die or make their transition. Say what you need to share from your heart and allow their Spirit to be healed, as mine was, upon my near-death. They will forever live in your heart. Let them go in peace, and cherish the time you had together. Allow them to die in dignity and with grace.

In the mid-1980s when I worked in the AIDS Community with men who were dying from AIDS complications, I recommended to them and their partners to come up with a special signal so when one of them died they would know they were fine.

Before my mom passed away, my entire family told my mom to make herself known during a holiday. A year after she died, at Christmas, my dad, a friend, and I were sitting in the front room of my dad's home. All of a sudden the lights went off and on three times. Dad and I smiled at each other. I had goose bumps, as my heart filled with joy. This was the signal my mom said she would give us. I ran into the bedroom to tell my sister, Joyce, and Jeaneen, and they were disappointed they didn't witness the lights blinking on and off. However, they too believed it was Mom. We all took time to share our love for her. Since then, Mom has made her presence known to us many times.

The veil is thin. Believe! The invisible realm is more real then the physical realm.

Eating Disorders

Society has placed so much importance on how you look, what you wear, and how much you weigh. People are dieting to fit in with society, magazines, models, and the fashion industry. Beauty is narrowly defined when it comes to our society. Cultural norms value people on their physical appearance, not their inner beauty and strengths. Men, women, and children allow appearances to dominate their lives. People are dying to look thin. Yes, dying! Females especially, but also males are dying needlessly due to eating disorders.

Estimates show 90% of all girls ages 3-11 have a Barbie doll, a role model with a figure unattainable in real life. Yet the image of Barbie is embedded in their minds. As they grow older and look through teen and women's magazines, they will be besieged with advertisements of stick-thin models selling various diets, diet foods and products.

At the age of 34, after getting out of my mentally and emotionally abusive marriage, I became anorexic. Within a matter of five months, I went from being physically healthy to weighing a meager 98 pounds. Anorexia gave me the power and control over something in my life.

Anorexia Nervosa is an eating disorder that came about when I first listened to and believed Bill's criticisms: I was fat, ugly, worthless, useless, a disgrace, and incompetent. He ridiculed everything I did or said. I started to limit my intake of food so I could lose weight (even though I was a size 10). Unexpressed emotions from my husband's verbal abuse and the memories of being raped by my grandfather were eating me alive.

After Bill and I divorced, I became so sick and weak I could no longer care for my daughter. I sent Jeaneen, then nine years old, to live with my parents, her father, and his parents who all lived in Maui, Hawaii. The guilt of sending Jeaneen away set in, yet I knew it was best for her. After she was in a safe place and I knew she was being treated well, I continued to starve myself, stayed in isolation, and sat in the house with the curtains drawn. I allowed unexpressed emotions and anorexia to eat my body, mind, and spirit. My mind had been so overwhelmed by abuse, I decided the only way to stop my suffering was to end my life.

My first attempt at suicide was unsuccessful—I threw up the full bottle of pills I had swallowed. A few days later, I leaned against the bathroom tub and placed a sharp, shiny razor on my left wrist. I said my final prayers and asked Infinite Spirit to forgive me for what I was about to do and to let me know if there was anything I needed to know before I killed myself. Instantly the entire bathroom filled up with magnificent, brilliant, warm, loving light from God. Telepathically, I heard, *"My Child, this is not your time to die. Get yourself into the hospital and when you return you will become a healer, teach around the world, and write books."*

None of this made sense to me but I knew without a doubt this was a message from God, and I had received my life purpose. I immediately allowed my doctor to admit me into an eating disorder hospital ward. He was relieved to get my call, as he had attempted to convince me for months to go into the hospital.

I wasn't the typical person with anorexia because I wasn't a teenager. I didn't weigh myself several times a day, do excessive exercise, or count calories. All I had to do was completely stop eating. I was diagnosed with anorexia because I experienced the following physical and emotional symptoms:

Anorexia Nervosa –

- ❖ Some of the physical signs are:
  Dramatic weight loss
  Fatigue
  Irregular heartbeats
  Constipation
  Loss of menstrual periods
  Bruises easily
  Overall weakness
  Dry skin
  Low blood pressure
  Dizziness
  Thin appearance
  Wearing baggy clothes
  Thin layers of hair on body, especially on face
  Dry hair and hair loss
  Brittle nails
  Always cold
  Difficulty sleeping
  Preoccupied with food
  Rearranging food on the plate
  Excessive chewing
  Refuses to eat or makes excuses for not eating
  Nauseous at the smell of food

- ❖ Some of the emotional signs are:
  Depression
  Feelings of guilt
  Low self-esteem
  Difficulty concentrating
  Disassociation from friends and family

> Always feeling fat
> Refusal to admit losing so much weight
> Lack of interest or involvement in any activities
> Denial of the consequence of losing weight

I discovered part my anorexia had to do with being so filled with unexpressed emotions there was no room for food. I had to learn to feel my feelings and express my emotions.

Although I haven't experienced bulimia nervosa, or binge eating, I am including the signs and symptoms so others don't put their lives at risk due to any type of eating disorder.

Bulimia Nervosa appears in two ways, purging and non-purging. The person who purges first binges on food, and then gets rid of it with laxatives, diet pills, vomiting, or enemas. The non-purging person binges on food, and then self-starves to lose the weight put on with the binging. Both types can lead to death.

❖ Some signs of Bulimia are:
> Smell of vomit
> Discolored teeth
> Scars or calluses on the knuckles or hands
> Swelling of the cheeks or jaw area
> Fluctuation in weight
> Eating without being hungry
> Frequent trips to the bathroom after eating
> Disassociating from friends and activities

Some common medical complications and adverse effects are:
> Irregular heartbeat
> Tooth decay and sores in mouth
> Ruptured stomach or esophagus
> Swelling of hands and feet

Loss of menstrual periods
Bloating and abdominal pain
Broken blood vessels in the eyes
Constipation from overuse of laxatives

Binge Eating Disorder and Compulsive Overeating generate feelings of shame and a desire to hide. Sometimes people with these disorders become so good at hiding their illness, even close friends and loved ones don't know they are bingeing. Most people with serious binge eating problems eat unusually large amounts of food and feel their eating is out of control.

❖ People with binge eating disorder may show these traits:
Inability to stop eating
Eat large amounts of food rapidly
Hide or stockpile food to eat later in secret
Feel depressed or guilty after overeating

Some physical signs:
Diabetes
High blood pressure
Kidney and liver problems
High cholesterol
Decreased mobility

Binge eating is different from bulimia nervosa, because binge eaters don't purge, fast, or do strenuous exercises after they binge eat.

All eating disorders can lead to death. It is important to get the appropriate medical care and treatment. Even after seeking medical care, you may find yourself falling back into eating disorder patterns. Catch yourself immediately and get back on a healthy path. I have lived the consequences and now realize the "choices" I must make to stay healthy and true to myself . . . to live!

Eating disorders can cause death! Don't turn your back on someone whom you think might have an eating disorder. Also, if after reading about eating disorders you fall into any one of the categories, immediately seek medical help.

As Dr. Phil McGraw says, "You can't change what you don't acknowledge."

જ્જ ન્જ

The Upsets of Nausea

I was sick many days, nights, and months when nausea took over. I felt blessed and relieved when I discovered different ways to help settle my stomach, and I would like to share them with you.

- ❖ Peppermint essential oil can be very soothing for an upset stomach and effective in a short time. (If your body is extremely weak, peppermint may be too strong for you). Mix a small amount of peppermint essential oils into oil, such as almond, jojoba, or olive. Place four to six drops about two inches above your navel and rub it into your skin. If you don't like to use oils on your skin, mix a small amount of peppermint oil with a cream or lotion. Make sure you wash your hands with soap and water after you use the essential oil because peppermint will sting if you get it in your eyes. There are different brands of peppermint essential oils, such as Young Living, Simplers, Wyndmere, Aura Cacia, and NOW.

- ❖ Ginger is very soothing to the stomach. Make ginger tea by slicing pieces of ginger and boiling them in water. You can also purchase ginger tablets. St. Clair's has a tin of small organic ginger snaps tablets you can slowly dissolve in your mouth.

- ❖ Chamomile and peppermint teas can be calming for nausea.

❖ Chamomile, fennel, fenugreek, goldenseal, papaya, and peppermint are good herbs for indigestion. Caution–do not use chamomile on an ongoing basis, and avoid it completely if you are allergic to ragweed. Do not take goldenseal internally on a daily basis for more than one week. Do not use it during pregnancy. It is also suggested to use these with caution if you are allergic to ragweed.

❖ Bach Flower Essence Rescue Remedy can also "quiet" an upset stomach.

❖ Acupuncture and acupressure points on the hands, ears, and feet can stop nausea.

❧　❦

Cleansing the Body

Hippocrates, known as the father of medicine, taught: "Wholesome natural food could restore health. The human body is self-regenerating and self-cleansing and, when given the proper tools with which to work, can maintain its natural state of well-being."

When I first came down with symptoms associated with HIV, I had to look at my lifestyle: eating habits, thoughts, actions, beliefs, and spirituality. For several years I worked on my thought patterns, my beliefs, and many more years on my spirituality. However, when it came to eating habits, I needed to start at the beginning.

I was a classic junk food, fast food, processed food eater. I didn't cook real meals or eat raw foods. When my body weakened, I realized I needed to detoxify it and find a new approach to eating. I enrolled in a three-week treatment program of detoxification, nutrition, enemas implants, and classes. In the classes I learned about the mind-body-spirit connection.

Much of what was taught in the mind and spirit classes I already knew and had been teaching others (a lot of which is included in this book). However, when it came to eating correctly, I felt like a baby learning something new. I cleansed my body through a live raw-food diet, lymphatic exercise, the consumption of wheatgrass juice, and colon therapy.

Going from junk food to only raw food was a shock to my body. I experienced several days of withdrawals, which showed up as headaches, nausea, and anger. However, once my body adjusted to the raw foods and wheatgrass, I felt energized, focused, and lighter.

I know there are many doctors who disagree with colon therapy or colonics, but there are also health authorities who believe disease begins in the colon. Dr. Bernard Jensen states, "Every tissue is fed by the blood, which is supplied by the bowel. When the bowel is dirty, the blood is dirty." For me colon therapy was extremely instrumental in my rapid healing process, as it helped me get rid of the toxins. After each colonic session, I was implanted with wheatgrass to absorb the minerals, vitamins, amino acids, and enzymes into the colon.

Wheatgrass juice (drinking and implants) is one substance I would definitely take if I became ill. It converts primary sun-food directly into chlorophyll and contains an abundance of vitamins, minerals, enzymes, and amino acids, all of which enhance and optimize your health and well-being. Wheatgrass resembles the hemoglobin in your blood. It is proven to boost the immune system and improve health.

After my three-week treatment, I felt my life was in balance and harmony, and I was no longer going to neglect or abuse my body with toxic foods.

For six months I stayed on the raw-food program at home, listened to my body through meditation and muscle testing, and slowly started to incorporate steamed vegetables, fruits, grains, fish, and chicken. My body no longer wanted or needed only raw foods.

Each body is unique. Listen to what it needs or wants. You can learn to do that through the instructions in this chapter, sub-chapter "Your Body Knows What It Wants and Needs." Also, seek advice from your health professionals.

❖ If you remove any of the following items from your diet your body doesn't have to work so hard: caffeine, sugar, alcohol, gluten breads, and animal products such as dairy, meats, and chicken.

I discovered, like so many other men and women, I was allergic to wheat and dairy. When I eliminated these two items from my diet I stopped feeling bloated, congested, and constipated.

❖ Another way I have cleansed my body (when my body told me to) was through juicing and fasting. I found even if I juiced or fasted for only three days, my body felt better. Three books I found valuable are:

Juicing for Life: A Guide to the Benefits of Fresh Fruit and Vegetable Juicing by Cherie Calbom.

Cherie and John Calbom also published *Juicing, Fasting and Detoxing for Life: Unleash the Healing Power of Fresh Juices and Cleansing Diets.*

Juice Fasting and Detoxification: Use the Healing Power of Fresh Juice to Feel Young and Look Great by Steve Meyerowitz.

❖ From time to time I have used the Arise and Shine Cleanse Program and *The Cleanse Cookbook* by Christine Dreher, CCN, CCH which is filled with delicious and healthy recipes. Christine discusses the importance of a balanced pH level in *The Cleanse Cookbook.*

To summarize, Christine states, "What is a balanced pH? The pH level is measured on a scale of 0 to 14. The mid point, 7, is considered to be neutral; above 7 is alkaline and below 7 is acidic. The higher the number, the more alkaline, the lower the number the more acidic.

There are many factors that affect pH levels. Eating acidic foods, high stress levels, extreme exercise, and shallow breathing will cause one's pH level to become more acidic. The best time of the day to test pH levels is the first thing in the morning before eating or drinking anything.

There are three ways you can test your pH—saliva test, urine test, and lemon test. pH paper (pHydrion papers work well) can be purchased at most health food stores and drug stores. The ideal range is 7.0 or higher, indicating your body has a good supply of alkaline minerals and is eliminating the excess through the urine.

6.5 to 6.9 indicates some depletion of alkaline minerals, though not serious.

5.6 to 6.4 indicates depletion of alkaline minerals that is more serious. It is suggested to replenish your alkaline reserves by eating a diet rich in alkaline-forming foods.

5.5 and below indicates that the body is very depleted and has no alkaline reserves. Replenish your alkaline reserves before attempting any cleanse program. Both cleansing and replenishing electrolytes can help balance pH levels."

The Cleanse Cookbook has healthy recipes for cleansing and detoxification, to bring your body back into the proper pH balance. For more information about Christine, cleansing, pH, and *The Cleanse Cookbook,* visit Christine's website at http://www.TransformYourHealth.com.

❖ *The pH Miracle for Weight Loss* by Robert and Shelley Young has a comprehensive, clear overview of the benefits of going alkaline and a simple program to alkalize your body, including exercise, supplements, and foods.

ॐ   ॐ

Informative Books

❖ Many health food stores and libraries carry a book entitled, *Alternative Medicine – The Definitive Guide*, compiled by The Burton Goldberg Group, which explains 350 leading-edge physicians' treatments. Within the 1,068 pages you will find Part One: The Future of Medicine, Part Two: Alternative Therapies, Part Three: Health Conditions, plus a Glossary of Medical Terms, Illustrations of Body Systems, Appendix, Endnotes, and an Index. The *Alternative Medicine—The Definitive Guide* book is a source of valuable information and resources.

❖ Most health food stores carry a book entitled, *Prescriptions for Nutritional Healing* by Phyllis A. Balch, which covers topics such as Understanding the Elements of Health, Disorders, Remedies and Therapies, and Appendix. If you don't want to purchase this book, you can look through the store copy for any suggested treatments and remedies for your disorder.

THE SPIRIT

❧　❦

Another Word for God

Every person has their own connection which speaks to their spirit, soul, and heart. Throughout this book I have used the word God and Infinite Spirit, as they are among the many words I call my source of life and the Creator of All. There are hundreds of words that can replace the word God such as Lord, Almighty, Supreme Being, Buddha, Great Spirit, Deity, Creator, Godhead, Omnipotent, Omniscient, All Merciful, Higher Power, Divine, Goddess, Tao, Holy One, Allah, Elohim, Yahweh, Kadosh, and the Alpha and Omega. As you read through this chapter where I have used the word *God* or *Infinite Spirit,* replace it with whatever word resonates with you.

I believe there is only One Power and Presence with many names.

Some people believe God to be in form, and other people believe God to be energy. Perhaps God is beyond names and form.

Joseph Campbell states in *The Mask of Eternity,* "God's center is everywhere and circumference nowhere. The center where you are is in each one a manifestation of that mystery." He goes on to say, "You are God in your deepest identity. You are one with the transcendent."

❧   ❧

Angels, Archangels, and Spirit Guides

Angels are among us. Indeed they are!

I believe every person has a Guardian Angel. Your angel's love is unconditional and your Guardian Angel is with you from your birth until you die. This angel has never been in a human body and has a high vibration energy frequency.

There are hundreds of Celestial Beings waiting to assist you on your journey.

When I was working on this sub-chapter, I went into a bookstore and looked through various books but couldn't find what I needed. Vira Cocha (one of my Master Teachers on the Spirit realm) assured me the book was there. The sales woman, whom I know, Leslie, directed me to a special order book that had just arrived a few days earlier. She allowed me to look though it, and when I opened the book, I gave thanks knowing it was perfect. Fortunately, the store had another copy, which I purchased, and then I contacted the author.

The book is *The Encyclopedia of Angels, Spirit Guides and Ascended Masters: A Guide to 200 Celestial Beings to Help, Heal, and Assist You in Everyday Life.* Author Susan Gregg has done extensive research with each of the 200 Celestial Beings—from different cultures, traditions, and beliefs. She has outlined their ways to assist you, including an invocation, and shares the background of each of these wonderful Beings of Light. Included are some beautiful watercolor drawings of the various angels, saints, and ascended masters. Through Susan's book, I was introduced to new wisdom, and the gifts, love, and endless compassion these Beings have to offer.

Ascended Masters, and Spirit Guides – Ascended Masters are people who became enlightened while on the Earth Plane and have chosen to continue to serve humanity after their ascension. Spirit Guides act as guides and are similar to your Guardian Angels. Spirit Guides have a deep connection to God and can perform miracles.

Master Teachers love to teach people and help them let go of their limiting beliefs. Some of these people are: Abraham, Afra, Babaji, Buddha, Confucius, Enoch, Jesus, John the Baptist, Lady of Guadalupe, Lady Nada, Lanto, Lao-tze, Mahatma Gandhi, Mary Magdalene, Melchizedek, Merlin, Moses, Mother Mary, Mother Teresa, Muhammad, Sai Baba, Sri Swami Satchidananda, Shiva, Solomon, White Buffalo Woman, White Fire Eagle, and Paramahansa Yogananda. All of them have the unique qualities of love, grace, and compassion.

Some people call the above category Masters of Light. Light-workers are workers of Light no matter the name.

There are also Archangels, such as Ariel, Chamuel, Gabriel, Haniel, Hasmal, Israfil, Jophiel, Laylah, Metatron, Michael, Ohrmazd, Pathiel, Raphael, Remiel, Sandalphon, Theliel, Uriel and Zadkiel. Archangels supervise guardian angels and the angels upon the earth.

Gods, Goddesses, and Deities – Each has been honored in a way that is consistent with their cultures. Some of them are: Aine, Altjira, Apollo, Blodeuwedd, Brahma, Cupid, Demeter, Enki, Great Spirit, Hina, Horus, Inanna, Inti, Ishtar, Isis, Itzamna, Ixchel, Krishna, Kwan Yin, Laima, Lakshmi, Lilith, Maeve, Mary, Morrigan, Mukuru, Namahoa Ke Ka'i, Odin, Oshun,

Pachamama, Pele, Perkunas, Quetzalcoatl, Ra, Sedna, Shiva, Tara, Thor, Vakarine, Venus, Vishnu, Wakan Tanka, Wandjina, and Yemaya.

Some of the Saints are: Agatha, Agnes of Assisi, Anthony of Padua, Brigid of Ireland, Bridget of Sweden, Cecelia, Christopher, Francis of Assisi, John of the Cross, Joseph, Nicholas, Padre Pio, and Patrick.

There are hundreds of highly evolved Celestial Beings on the spirit realm to assist you, but they cannot help until you specifically call upon them.

I would like to introduce you to the Celestial Beings who have assisted me on my journey.

- ❖ My first encounter with the spirit realm was at the age of three. Throughout the nine years of being raped by my grandfather, an Angel appeared before me. I could see her, yet I could see through her. As I was being abused, she lifted me out of my body and took me somewhere special. She told me she was my angel and she was here to teach me love. She taught me how to communicate with the other kingdoms (plant, mineral, animal, human, and spirit). She showed me how we are all connected and told me we are not separate from God. I learned that as I connected with my wholeness, I was in touch with my holiness. To this day, I still see and talk to this angel and call upon her. She is my Angel of Love.

- ❖ When I was in the hospital with anorexia in 1984, I started to hear an unfamiliar male voice. He spoke with immense compassion and love. I listened attentively to what was said and could understand with a clarity that I never had before. I was told to write down everything I heard. All

186

the questions I had and the answers I received were signed "Vira Cocha." I never questioned who was speaking. I accepted it, because the messages were profound and loving.

When I felt Vira Cocha's presence and heard his voice, a deep sense of inner peace filled my soul, and my heart relaxed into a state I had never felt before. A state of magnificent love. I have never seen Vira Cocha, but I know his Spirit as one of my Master Teachers of Light.

A few years later Vira Cocha recommended I attend a workshop with Brooke Medicine Eagle. Vira Cocha told me to go up to her at the end of the seminar because she had a message for me. I did as instructed. At first, she looked puzzled and said she had no idea what the message was. About five minutes later she came up to me and said, "I am told you are supposed to read *He Walked the Americas.*" I graciously thanked her and immediately went out and bought the book, written by L. Taylor Hansen. In the chapters written from Peru, I learned about Vira Cocha as being a Prophet, like Jesus. In Peru, Wiracoch or Vira Cocha is considered the Creator of All.

Vira Cocha will be with me forever!

❖ During that same time in the hospital, an old Japanese man about 4'9", with a long white beard and tall staff, stood before my bed and said he was here to teach me about Eastern healing therapies and philosophies. His name is Semitar. He is a very wise man with NO sense of humor. From 1984 to 1999 Semitar was with me. When I went to Peru in 1999, he told me I no longer needed him, as I had learned all he was here to teach me. He said another spiritual teacher would come to me before long.

When Semitar left, I felt like I had lost one of my best friends.

❖ Onaca has been with me since 2002. I don't see her, but I feel her loving presence and hear her words. She is here to assist me and support my writing.

❖ Another Celestial Being I resonate with is Lazaris. From 1984 to 1995, in Los Angeles, I had an opportunity to attend most of Lazaris's workshops. Lazaris is a non-physical entity. He is a consciousness without form, and has never chosen to take human form.

Since 1974, Lazaris has channeled through Jach Pursel, his only channel, offering his friendship and love, and generating a remarkable body of tools, techniques, processes, and pathways for our Spiritual Journey to God/ Goddess/All That Is.

In person or through CDs, Lazaris captivates me with love, wisdom, and soft-spoken words through the presentations and meditations, and I feel cocooned in a bright Light of Love.

To learn more about Lazaris, the workshops, and CDs visit http://www.lazaris.com.

Yes, we all have angels, archangels, and spirit guides, those celestial beings who are here to assist us. All you have to do is call upon them. You don't have to do anything alone. The most important point to remember is they cannot interfere with your life or help you unless you call upon them and ask for assistance, guidance, or support.

I would like to share with you a process I do and have taught people on how to get in touch with their angels or spirit guides. Trust what you hear when you listen, even if you cannot describe it.

1. Before you begin your visualization, I want you to know whatever you receive is appropriate. Drop all sense of unworthiness. You may see a light, someone familiar, a figure you can see through (angel or spirit being), an animal, or you may see nothing at all, but feel a presence of some thing or someone.

2. Find a comfortable setting, indoors or out. Allow yourself to get in a comfortable position. Gently close your eyes. Take in a few slow deep breaths in through your nose, and as you exhale, let out a sigh from your mouth. If you hear any noise, allow the noise to let you go deeper and become more relaxed. Ask to set aside your ego, and let go of any thoughts, fears, and concerns. Ask only that which is truly for your highest good in Divine law and order, or love and light, be revealed to you.

3. Imagine walking down a path. Create the path any way you want. It might lead into a forest, meadow, or the beach. Create the path you desire. Notice what you create as you walk down this path. Perhaps there are trees, birds, a stream, or flowers. Whatever you create is perfect. Notice if there are any sounds. Feel safe and secure as you continue to walk down this path. Continue to notice what you see, feel, hear, and perhaps smell.

4. Now notice in the distance there is a beautiful, bright, and magnificent Light. This Light is brilliant. You feel drawn to this Light. You feel peace, love, and comfort as you continue to walk toward this Light.

5. As you walk closer to this Light, perhaps you can see an image of a Being, a man, or woman known or unknown to you, an angel, or perhaps you see an animal. If all you see is the Light that is fine.

6. Thank this Light, Being, or animal for coming to you. Feel the power, presence, and love come toward you.

7. Then ask, "What is your name?"

   Take the very first words that come to your mind. Don't question it.

8. Ask, "What are you here to teach me?"

   Listen.

9. Then ask, "How long have you been with me?"

   Listen.

10. Ask, "What talents, gifts, or message want to be expressed through me?"

    Listen. It may surprise you. If you don't understand completely, ask for more details. If you hear, "Your talent is in communication," ask a question such as: communication in what way?

11. Ask, "What is my life purpose?"

    Listen.

12. Then ask, "What wisdom, knowledge, or qualities do I need to manifest in order to fulfill my life purpose?"

Once again, listen.

13. Ask, "What do I need to let go of that no longer serves me?"

Listen.

14. Then feel free to ask questions about any area of your life, such as health, relationships, or anything from your heart. If you don't receive your answer, know within three days you will. The answers may come to you through various ways such as another person, a song, something you read, or a dream. Just be open to receiving the answers to your questions.

15. Once again ask, "Is there anything else I need to hear at this time concerning my questions?"

Listen.

16. This Light, Being, or totem animal has a gift for you. Notice if you can see it. If not, that's fine. Thank this Light or Being for the gift.

17. Ask, "How do you want me to use this gift?"

Then give thanks.

18. Ask the Light, Being, or totem animal, "How would you like me to communicate with you and how often?"

Listen. You might hear through visualization, writing, meditation, being out in nature, or everyday activities. Whatever you hear is perfect for you.

19. Ask the Light, Being, or animal once again, "Is there anything else you want to tell me or I need to know at this time?"

Listen.

20. Thank this Light, Being, or animal for coming to you and for being your angel or guide.

21. Imagine yourself gently cradled in the Light and love of this Being or animal. Feel a deep sense of love around and through you.

22. Now tell this Light, Celestial Being, or animal you are going back down the path and notice if they leave, stay with you, or follow you.

Whatever happens is perfect.

23. Begin to walk back down the path you created, feeling more alive, peaceful, and loved. As you continue to walk down your path to the end, notice if there are new things being created as you walk.

24. When you get to the end of your path, turn around and place your hands in a prayer-like position at your heart chakra, and bow your head in gratitude.

25. Bring this loving energy back into your body. Now take a deep breath in through your nose and exhale through your mouth. Begin to notice the outside noises around you. Feel your body and slowly move your hands and feet. When you feel comfortable, gently open your eyes.

When you have completed your visualization, while it is still fresh in your mind, you may want to write down everything you remember and experienced.

The more often you connect with your angel, spirit guide, animal totem, or Light, the stronger the voice and presence will be.

If you find it difficult to hear your angel or spirit guide, quiet your mind, set aside your ego and fears, and ask that you write the highest truth in love and light. Ask your questions then write down everything you hear in your mind. Once you start writing, you may notice the voice. I first became familiar with Vira Cocha teachings through writing, and now I know his voice as well as my own. I no longer need to write. Don't be surprised if you hear or write words you usually don't use. Celestial Beings all have their own personalities. I have one friend who can tell when her spirit guide is around because she smells his pipe and hears his British accent.

If your Angel or Spirit Guide talks too fast, ask them to slow down. Also, if you need clarification it is important to ask for it.

If you haven't experienced the Spirit Realm, I would like to suggest you open your heart and mind to a beautiful, new journey through life. There are many helpful books and tools to assist you to feel connected to this kingdom.

❖ Shakti Gawain's *Creative Visualization: Use the Power of Your Imagination to Create What You Want In Your Life.* I read Shakti Gawain's book in 1985, and it opened up so many possibilities to my life. I highly recommend her book to everyone.

❖ Susan Gregg's previously mentioned book, *The Encyclopedia of Angels, Spirit Guides and Ascended*

Masters: A Guide to 200 Celestial Beings to Help, Heal, and Assist You in Everyday Life.

❖ *Angelspeake: How to Talk with Your Angels* is a simple introductory book, written by Barbara Mark and Trudy Griswold, which includes easy communication techniques.

❖ Doreen Virtue, Ph.D, has an excellent variety of books, CDs, and oracle cards filled with information about Angels. I have purchased several of her items, including her 44 card deck and guidebook entitled *Messages from Your Angels,* and *Goddess Guidance Oracle Cards* with specific messages and beautiful artwork.

❖ Sylvia Browne is a well–known author and has valuable information in her book titled, *Book of Angels.*

❖ *Ask Your Angels* is a practical guidebook to work with the messengers of heaven on ways to empower and enrich your life. The authors of *Ask Your Angels* are Alma Daniel, Timothy Wyllie, and Andrew Ramer.

❖ Meredith L. Young–Sowers has a magical book and card set entitled *Angelic Messenger CARDS—A Divination System for Spiritual Self-Discovery.* I shuffle the cards and while I mix them up, I think of my question. Then I ask my question and without looking pick a card. It is amazing how I am drawn to the card I need. If I don't have a particular question I ask, "What do you want to tell me at this time?" or "What wisdom do you want to share with me?"

If you think you might be hearing your Angel or Spirit Guides, you are! It may come across as your intuition.

❧ ❧

Auras

Everything has an aura. Everyone is surrounded by an electro-magnetic field called an aura. An aura is a luminous energy field that emanates from an object or your body. Your aura is a protective shield that keeps you healthy. However, the state of your health, diet, mood, stress, emotions, and surroundings may adversely affect your aura and govern the intensity of the color. Generally the aura is a mixture of various colors, but every person has a distinctive shade that denotes their personality. Your aura is in a constant state of movement. It can be a few inches to many feet in all directions from your body.

Some people are gifted to see the colors of auras, while others are blessed to see the energy patterns. These people can help you be aware of what health issues and problems may arise regarding your well-being. They can also cleanse your aura and show you how to do it yourself.

As I look at people and objects, I usually don't see auras. However, I have practiced the following exercise which has allowed me to see auras for a few seconds:

1. Have a friend or loved one stand in front of a white background, such as a white wall or white construction board. Have them stand facing you or sideways so you are looking at their side. It is best to do this in daylight because the sun's rays are full spectrum.

   I do this outside, in front of a garage and have someone hold up the white board.

2. Relax your eyes. Make sure you don't strain them. You may want to look beyond your subject and let your eyes go a little out of focus.

3. Look at the person for a minute or so. You will begin to see the various energies and colors.

4. The colors may disappear within a few seconds.

5. You may find after you have held the white board up and looked at the person for a minute or so, then pulled the white board away, you will see the aura for a longer period of time.

You can also catch a glimpse of your aura by looking into the mirror.

1. Use a soft background light or a little bit of light coming in from the window, but not bright light.

2. Face the mirror with a white background behind you.

3. As you look into the mirror, relax your eyes, looking at your head and shoulders.

4. Let your eyes look beyond yourself, at the wall behind you.

5. You will begin to see energy and perhaps colors around the top and sides of your head.

6. Your aura may disappear quickly, but you can always begin the steps again.

It is interesting to check your aura as you go through different situations and emotions.

In The Body Chapter, sub-chapter "The Use of Energy," there are a couple of exercises where you will feel the energy of the auras.

There is also the Seven Layers of the Auric Body System which is listed below.

The first three are associated with the physical plane.

1. The Etheric Body (lower etheric aspect) is about ¼ inch to 2 inches beyond your physical body. This is your layer of physical health.

2. The Emotional Body (lower emotional aspect) is approximately 1 to 3 inches from your physical body. This is the storehouse of emotions.

3. The Mental Body (lower mental aspect) is 3 to 8 inches from your body. This has to do with power and relationships.

4. The Astral Body is associated with the heart. It is ½ feet to 1½ feet from your physical body. The Astral Body deals with matters of love. It also provides a link between mind-body-spirit and connects you with all living Beings. This is the astral plane bridge.

The last three bodies are associated with the spirit plane.

5. The Etheric Template is 1½ feet to 2 feet from your body. It is the energy field of communication and creative expression.

6. The Celestial Body is 2 feet to 3½ feet from your body. It represents the visual senses. It also reflects your view of the world.

7. The Causal Body or Ketheric Template is 3½ to 4 feet from your physical body. This is your Divine Connection, Higher Self.

All seven of these bodies are a vehicle to guide and support us through this lifetime.

Barbara Ann Brennan's book, *Hands of Light: A Guide to Healing Through the Human Energy Field* is filled with valuable information about the bodies, auric layers, and energy, and provides exercises, illustrations, and healing methods. This book has been popular since the mid-1980s, and will continue to be used by people in the healing fields for decades.

❧   ❧

The Seven Main Chakras

In 1985, my mentor, Linda, was the first person to educate me about chakras. She had a large, colorful chart in her office that explained the different chakras (pronounced chahkruh), which is a Sanskrit word meaning "wheel."

Everyone has chakras whether you are aware of them or not. Sometimes called the "wheel of life," a chakra is a wheel-like vortex which exists in the surface of your etheric body. Chakras are like the pathways from the energy bodies to the physical body. Your chakras are always active, but sometimes they become weak. As you start from your bottom chakra and work your way up, they rotate in alternating order.

As you read about the various chakras, begin to notice if you have had health issues in one or more of the chakras. Once you are aware of which chakras are weak, you can strengthen them.

Listed below are the seven main chakras. Please note, there are more chakras, but these are the seven most people are familiar with. The information I have gathered throughout the decades on chakras comes from various sources, so you may discover different and additional information from other books.

❖ The First Chakra – The Root Chakra
Location: Base of the spine or tailbone
Color: Red
Element: Earth
Associated Gland: Adrenal – Controls body solids, such
as the spinal column, bones, teeth, and nails. Also

the blood, the building process of cells, the colon, and the rectal area.

Some Qualities: Survival, power to achieve goals, vitality, grounded to Mother Earth, security, stability, will to live, and courage.

Affirmations: My Spirit is grounded in my body.

❖ The Second Chakra – The Sacral/Spleen Chakra
Location: Below the navel
Color: Orange
Element: Water
Associated Organs: Reproductive organs, kidneys, and bladder.
Some Qualities: Sexual energy, creativity, money, and guilt.
Affirmation: I embrace my life with creativity and passion.

❖ The Third Chakra – The Solar Plexus Chakra
Location: Above the navel and below the chest
Color: Yellow
Element: Fire
Associated Organs: Pancreas, liver, stomach, spleen, gall bladder, autonomic nervous system, lower back, and also muscles.
Some Qualities: Personal power, authority, self-control, social identity, influence, anger, and betrayal.
Affirmation: I use my personal power in a balanced way.

❖ The Fourth Chakra – The Heart Chakra
Location: The center of the chest
Color: Green
Element: Air

Associated Gland: Thymus – Controls the heart, blood circulation, immune system, lower lungs, rib cage, skin, and upper back.

Some Qualities: Forgiveness, compassion, understanding, harmony, healing, nurturing, love, giving, and receiving.

Affirmation: I feel compassion and love.

❖ The Fifth Chakra – The Throat Chakra
Location: The throat area
Color: Blue
Element: Ether
Associated Gland: Thyroid – controls the jaw, neck, throat, voice, airways, upper lungs, and arms.
Some Qualities: Self-expression, creativity, inspiration, communication, and individual will.
Affirmation: I communicate clearly and speak my truth confidently.

❖ The Sixth Chakra – The Third Eye Chakra
Location: Middle of the forehead
Color: Indigo
Element: Light
Associated Gland: Pituitary – Controls the endocrine system, the left brain hemisphere, the left eye, nose, ears, sinuses, and parts of the nervous system.
Some Qualities: Intuition, clairvoyance, insight, peace of mind, and will to know the truth.
Affirmation: I see with clear vision, intuition, and wisdom.

❖ The Seventh Chakra – The Crown Chakra
Location: The top and center of the head
Color: Violet

Element: Thought

Associated Gland: Pineal – controls cerebrum, right brain hemisphere, right eye, central and nervous systems

Some Qualities: Unity with the Divine, wisdom and purpose, spiritual awareness, and universal consciousness.

Affirmations: I am One with Spirit. Spirit flows through me.

Most people don't talk about other chakras, however, there are more. The Eight Chakra, is above the head, contains our life's purpose, and represents our contract or agreement for this lifetime. The sound for the eight and above chakras would be silence.

Because of sexual abuse, most of my lower chakras were weak. My Throat Chakra, the fifth chakra, was also weak, which made it difficult to express myself. However, once I became familiar with the different chakras, I was able to do energy work which cleared and strengthened the weak chakras.

❖ There is a beautiful book by Liz Simpson, *The Book of Chakra Healing,* that shows you how to work with the chakras, the archetypes, and also presents exercises, meditations, affirmations, and visualizations associated with each chakra.

❖ One of the classic chakra books is *Wheels of Life: A Guide to the Chakra System* by Judith Anodea, PhD. This book has extensive information about the chakras and things associated with each chakra such as vowel sounds, metals, foods, senses, planets, and much more.

The Differences Between Your Soul and Spirit

Mankind is made up of the material and the immaterial. Your "soul" is embodied within you. Your soul is in many ways your life and it is subjective to your spirit. It is a doer of the will and spirit. Your soul is a reflection of spirit.

Your "spirit," however, is ethereal and not physical. Your spirit is your true essence of love, light, truth, and wisdom. Your spirit is your center, and at your center is where you experience tranquility, balance, serenity, harmony, love, wholeness, and peace. Your spirit is undivided and the essence of all—I Am.

Through the soul and spirit you have the capacity to experience and express Divine Love while living on the earth plane.

On the Internet, at http://www.ask.com, when I typed in the question, "What is the difference between your soul and spirit," it stated "The 'soul' and the 'spirit' are similar in the manner in which they are used in the spiritual life of the believer. They are different in their reference. The 'soul' is man's horizontal view with the world. The 'spirit' is man's vertical view with God. It is important to understand that both refer to the immaterial part of man, but only the 'spirit' refers to man's walk with God. The 'soul' refers to man's walk in the world, both material and immaterial."

I agree with the definition the Internet has to offer on the difference between your soul and spirit.

Spirituality versus Religion

To me, spirituality is personal, felt within my heart, and it brings about a sense of inner peace and security. I used to think religion was spirituality, but after many years of searching for what was true within the core of my Being (that part of me that knows the highest truth of who I am and knows only my highest good), I found spirituality.

The word spirituality can mean religion, theology, or mysticism. What I found is a higher truth separate from rules and dogma. I realize now I am and always have been whole and complete.

This kind of Beingness is not based on boundaries, judgment, rules, favoritism, or condemnation. It is based on the connection and Oneness with All. It is honoring this connection between all that is visible or invisible. It is embracing and knowing the God presence within all and that there is no separation. By embracing my own wholeness I am living my authentic life.

I grew up Catholic and at one time thought about being a Good Shepherd Nun, where I would work with troubled teenage girls. Then one day I missed mass and was told I was going to go to Hell. That was a turning point in my life. The thought I would be banished to a place called "hell" for missing one hour of mass didn't fit with the All-Loving Creator who spoke to me in my heart. Right then I knew I could no longer participate in a creed so removed from my concept of a loving God within. I see the Divinity in the world and experience the perfection in everyone and everything.

In my search for the truth I began to study self-awareness which resonated and expanded my consciousness of the connection and effect on the One Presence. I honor all Spiritual traditions, knowing the Universal Truth blends and weaves among all religions—God is all there is.

I became a New Thought Minister in 1986, and I am in accord with the truth at the center of all religions. However, I have witnessed a lot of religions that are dualistic and designed to maintain control over the communities they serve. This no longer works for me. We are all equal, and one with God! There is no separation.

How peaceful, pure, beautiful, and loving it is to be able to experience Infinite Spirit within nature, within people, and within the center of who I am—the Divine Mystic inside me. Mysticism is a way of stepping into the mystery of life and allowing it to unfold for the highest good of all.

Prayer and Meditation

It doesn't matter what Higher Power or religion you adhere to, prayer and meditation allow a sense of peace and an opportunity to receive Divine information. Before I begin or end a prayer or meditation I always acknowledge the presence of the Divine (God, Infinite Spirit, Higher Power, Buddha, Universe) and give thanks.

Is there a difference between prayer and meditation? A lot of people say prayer is when you talk to God and meditation is when you listen to God. Both prayer and meditation can raise your consciousness and connect you to the Oneness of ALL.

❖ Prayer comes from within. Really feel what you are saying, whether you are talking out loud or silently to God. In prayer you may be seeking advice or direction, but it is important to remember that which you desire or seek may not be for your highest good. God's way is not always your way. In prayer always ask that it *"be for my highest good,"* or if other people are involved, ask that it *"be for the highest good of all concerned."*

Prayer doesn't have to be in a religious or spiritual setting. Prayer can be anywhere, for Infinite Spirit is everywhere. Some of my most heartfelt prayers are spoken when I am out in nature. Not only am I feeling a connection to nature, but to all the essences of the Creator.

Prayer can take many forms such as chanting, singing, walking, or sitting.

❖ Meditation is an ancient practice. It is about turning your attention within and letting go of your daily thoughts and activities. It is a feeling of inner peace as you connect with Infinite Spirit and make yourself available to receive higher wisdom. Meditation can relieve stress, promote relaxation, and improve your outlook. It is about waking up to life, to all its choices and possibilities.

There are different forms of meditation such as Transcendental Meditation, Mindful Meditation, Zen Meditation, Taoist Meditation, and Buddhist Meditation.

Some are concentrative meditations and others are mindful meditations. If you would like to learn about the different forms of meditation, there are countless books available, or go on the Internet and search "Types of Meditation."

❖ Meditation is when I quiet my busy mind and listen to Infinite Spirit or the stillness. When you meditate, you are learning to hear the still small voice that comes from deep within and to listen to Divine Guidance. In the stillness hear the voice of God and know your inner voice will always tell you the truth.

When I start meditation, I find a comfortable place indoors or outdoors, and take a few slow deep breaths. I set aside my fears, ego, and concerns to hear the Divine truth. I gently close my eyes and let go of any outside noises. If I have a question, I state it and listen for an answer.

After I have become centered and quieted my mind, what I have found helpful is to ask, "What do you want to tell me?" As I tap into my inner wisdom, the guidance and advice come to me quickly and profoundly. It is as if flood gates are opened with information, just by asking the simple question, "What do you want to tell me?"

❖ Another form of mediation I use is Mindful Meditation. This is when you calm your mind and consciously focus your awareness on your breath, sensations, feelings, thoughts, sounds, smells, and listen. You attune yourself to your surroundings, inside and outside.

I remember once I was with a group of friends doing Mindful Meditation and was so attuned to the mindfulness, I heard a button fall on the floor across the room. I wasn't positive at the moment it was a button, but when we came out of the meditation, a lady said she lost the button off her jacket. I was able to tell her where it had rolled.

Another way I have used Mindful Meditation is at the beach. The first time was while participating in a vision quest with Joan Halifax in the Yucatan. Ever so slowly, I gently placed my foot on the ground, one inch at a time, being conscious of my connection to Mother Earth and the sacredness of each and every step and breath. It didn't matter how long it took. I felt a deep connection. When I attend Thich Nhat Nanh weekend retreats, I notice they practice mindful walks and meditations.

❖ More and more doctors are recommending meditation to their patients as a way to lower blood pressure, decrease heart rate, decrease respiration rate, decrease stress, relieve insomnia, and increase relaxation. Meditation is a safe and simple way to balance physical, emotional, and mental states.

The following is a very simple way to experience meditation using your breath. If you are new to meditation, at first you may hear chatter in your mind. However, before long you will become one with your breath.

1. Find a comfortable place where you won't be interrupted.

2. You can sit or lay down during your meditation. I prefer to sit. If you decide to sit up you may want to have your back flat against a straight chair and your legs and arms uncrossed. Or you may want to sit on the floor with your legs crossed like the Native American Indians do.

3. Find a comfortable position with your shoulders relaxed and your hands resting on your lap.

4. Gently close your eyes.

5. Take a deep slow relaxing breath in through your nose.

6. Let it out slowly, through your mouth.

7. Focus your attention on your breath.

8. Surrender your chatter.

9. Ask it to become quiet.

10. Shift your awareness to your breath.

11. Breathe in peace and relax your body, emotions, and mind.

12. As you exhale release any tension and notice the relaxation in and through your body.

13. Now focus your entire attention only on your breath.

14. If thoughts or chatter distract you, ask them to be quite and refocus on your breath.

15. Become one with your breath.

16. This is your breath of life and it is sacred.

17. Continue to focus your attention on your sacred breath for the next few minutes.

18. Take a deep slow breath and begin to become aware of your surroundings.

19. Then gently open your eyes.

20. Notice how you feel throughout your body—peaceful, calm, and relaxed.

You may find it difficult to focus on your breath at first, because the chatter in your mind doesn't like to be quiet. Whenever you mind pulls you away from your breath, just notice it and then bring your attention back to your breath. When you begin to meditate, set aside five minutes, and each time you meditate increase the amount of time. Before long you will look forward to the stillness of the mind and become one with your breath.

Meditation can be that simple!

Carl Gustav Jung writes, "Who looks outside, dreams; who looks inside, awakens."

In *Minding the Body, Mending the Mind*, Dr. Joan Borysenko, best-selling author and internationally-known speaker states, "Through meditation we can learn to access the relaxation response (the physiological response elicited by meditation) and to be aware of the mind and the way our attitudes produce stress. In addition, by quieting the mind, meditation can also put one in touch with the inner physician, allowing the body's own inner wisdom to be heard."

Joan's wisdom, inspiration, and healing come to life in several of her meditation CDs, *Meditations for Relaxation and Stress Reduction* and *Meditations for Self Healing and Inner Power.*

Bernie Siegel, MD, is a well-known best-selling author and presenter who has made a profound difference in the lives of people faced with illness, including mine. He has several CDs on meditations that can assist you to go deep into the essence of what are seeking.

1. *Meditations for Difficult Times*
2. *Meditations for Enhancing Your Immune System*
3. *Meditations for Finding the Key to Good Health* (Prescriptions for Living)
4. *Meditations for Morning and Evening* (Prescriptions for Living)
5. *Meditations for Peace of Mind* (Prescriptions for Living)

The brilliant poet, Rumi, shares in *The Illuminated Rumi,* "Essence is emptiness, everything else accidental. Emptiness brings peace to loving. Everything else, disease. In this world of trickery emptiness is what your soul wants."

Meditation can be as easy as focusing on your breath, a sound, a word (mantra), an image, or the expansion and awareness of everything.

211

Be still! You are a limitless Being of Light. Allow higher wisdom to flow to and through you.

Mantras

The word "*mantra*" comes from two Sanskrit words. "Man" means "manas" or "mind." The second syllable, "trai," means "to protect" or "to free from." In the most literal sense Mantra means "to free from the mind."

Mantras are energy-based sounds or phrases. As you repeat the words or sounds out loud, the vibration increases and you become part of the vibration. You expand beyond your mind and may find yourself in the essence of the cosmic existence.

❖ "OM" is a powerful mantra. The Buddhist and Hindu consider OM to be the supreme and most sacred syllable. OM consists in Sanskrit of three sounds, a, u, and m. It is believed to be the spoken essence of the Universe.

❖ "HU" is considered a love song to God. The word is pronounced "hue." Singing it enhances our connection to God. This mantra has been used to assist people to open up to their deeper spiritual potential and draw them closer to the essence of God.

You can purchase CDs with both of these mantras and play them throughout the day. I use Robert Slap's *Eternal OM* and Harold Klemp's *HU: A Love Song to God.*

Various religions and spiritual groups use mantras as a powerful tool to connect at a deeper level to God and all that is. Thomas Ashley-Farrand wrote a book, *Healing Mantras,* which explains how and why mantras work and how to use them for healing, insight, and spiritual growth. The words are translated from the original Sanskirt and Thomas explains the word, how to pronounce it, and the application.

You can also find a lot of mantras by doing a search on the Internet. Take the time to discover mantras that resonate with you and you will feel a sense of Oneness as you repeatedly say them.

Service to Humanity

Assisting and supporting another person or organization can be extremely rewarding. As a child, my parents encouraged my brothers, sister, and me to help others. There was an 80-year-old woman who lived across the street who was homebound. Her daughter took care of her. We helped them by taking care of their yard. In junior high, I volunteered in a children's mental home. I was assigned to work with a little girl for a year, and found great pleasure as I read to her, brushed her hair, held her in my arms, talked to her, took her on walks in her wheelchair, and massaged her hands, arms, and legs. When I was married and lived in Japan, I volunteered in a military hospital helping wounded men from Vietnam. I would write letters for them, listen to their words and feelings, massage their feet and hands (when possible), and just "Be" with them. When my daughter started grade school, I assisted in her classroom, and at school outings and special events.

In the late 1980s, after I healed my past, I had an opportunity to teach self-esteem classes at juvenile halls in Los Angeles. Then I was asked to teach ongoing classes in "Taking Charge of Your Life," at Camp Scott, which is a correctional facility for teenage girls. I was amazed at how eager these girls were to listen, learn, and show they really wanted to change their lives. For some of the young women, they just needed to be heard and shown appreciation for who they truly were, not for their behaviors or actions, but as a Being. Before I left, I had a waiting list of girls who desired to attend my workshops.

My largest amount of time was spent volunteering with the AIDS and cancer communities. In the late 1980s at Marianne Williamson's LA Center for Living, while Stuart Altschuler was the executive director, I taught visualization, stress reduction, meditation, body dialogue, affirmations, emotional clearing, energy work, and the importance of positive attitude. The mind-body-spirit techniques I had learned enhanced my own well-being and allowed me to heal my past, and I found it helpful to share the knowledge and experience with others. I also invited men who were infected with AIDS into my home and did hands-on-healing energy work on them.

I enjoyed educating men, women, and children about the myths and reality of HIV/AIDS. I spent countless hours serving on national and international boards of directors and planning councils, as well as getting involved with fundraisers and speaking engagements.

Jeaneen and I enjoyed some of our holidays making baskets for the patients in hospitals, and we also helped feed the homeless and those less fortunate.

In the early 1990s, I experienced the sacredness of life and death when I trained and volunteered with Project Nightlight in Los Angeles. I sat with men dying from AIDS complications. Cassandra Christenson's vision for Project Nightlight was to not allow any person to die alone. As a volunteer, I assisted patients at Carl Bean AIDS Care Center. I sat at men's bedsides, held their hands, prayed silently, and assisted them in whatever way I could.

There were so many amazing men, yet I remember one in particular. His name was Tony and he was Native American. Tony was thin and wasting. It was hard to hug him, he was so frail, yet whenever I visited he was eager to be hugged. I immediately felt a deep connection to Tony, and I believe he felt the same toward me. When I looked around his small one-bedroom apartment, I could tell he was proud of his traditions, culture, and ancestors. The photos of his friends, family members, and horses, and his drums and rattles were neatly placed around his bedroom. I could see the pain in his eyes, yet his love was brighter than his pain. Sometimes Tony would ask me to softly play his sacred drum, with the rhythm of the heartbeat. Other times I would sit in silence. My presence was to serve Tony in whatever way he needed—prop up his pillows, give him water through a straw, gently massage his hands and feet, adjust his skeletal body, read to him, wipe away his sweat with a cool damp cloth, pray, sit, and listen. Sometimes there would be silence for a long time, but his heart was still beating. Tony loved to have me hold his hand as he fell asleep. Even though Tony embraced his past, when he died, his family was not present at his final celebration. They missed a great gift. I was honored to be with Tony during his final days of life.

Richard was well-known in the AIDS Community, and I assisted him during his final days. I had known Richard for five years, and I sat down with him to create a unique memorial that represented his life story and final wishes. I felt blessed and honored when he asked me to officiate his final celebration.

One of the greatest gifts I have received from these men who died from AIDS complications was a profound feeling of love and compassion.

Volunteering has brought added meaning to my life.

When you freely volunteer your time, it is important to find an organization or club you believe in. It might be the Alzheimer's Association, Blind Institute, Hospice, Boy/Girl Scouts, church, a shelter, a food bank, an animal shelter, or Big Brother/Big Sister.

It doesn't matter where you volunteer; the important thing is you are giving your time and service to something you believe in.

A lot of times when someone dies, a loved one volunteers (after they have grieved) with an organization that assisted them during their difficult times. It seems to help in the recovery process to give back to others, and not sit and dwell upon their loss.

Besides your favorite club or organization, you may want to help someone closer to you. Your neighbor may need extra help, the homeless person on the street may need food or a new pair of shoes, a friend may need time away from their children, a homebound person may use your assistance to get things for them when you go to the store, or a friend may need help with the yard. You may want to give the gift of life by donating blood regularly and registering as an organ or tissue donor.

When you give yourself to another, your energy level will radiate with joy, love, and gratitude. Serve with passion and help others without expecting anything in return.

When you help another, there is a sense of connection and value. I believe service is a gift to humanity and God. How can you be of greater service? How can you nurture your fellowman?

Your Life Purpose

Throughout this world and universe there is no one like you. Snowflakes, grains of sand, or even identical twins are not exactly the same.

Before you were born into this physical Being, you chose your parents and the circumstances you needed to learn and grow into your truth and express it. You had within you, all along, talents or gifts to share with others. Those talents and gifts can manifest in hobbies and activities, and can also develop into careers. Within those talents and gifts may lie your life purpose. For example, being a teacher, artist, mechanic, landscaper, builder, photographer, health care provider, sales representative, chef, or veterinarian come from your innate gifts. Sometimes you might think cooking, traveling, playing with animals, or painting are just for fun, but your life purpose might lie within these hobbies of yours.

Some people know their life purpose when young, while others search for it, knowing what they are currently doing doesn't bring them passion and joy—a great indicator they aren't on the right path of their life purpose.

If you aren't sure of your life purpose, write a list of things that make you happy and uplifted, such as being around people, being in nature, working with numbers, educating children, traveling, or building. Then think of the ideal environment. See yourself surrounded by people with personalities you enjoy. Start to really focus on what lights up your life, heart, and eyes when you think about it or do it. This is probably your life purpose, or related to it. Let it be ignited.

If you're still not sure of your life purpose, do any of the visualizations throughout The Spirit Chapter and ask God, your Angel, or Spirit Guide to clearly show you your life purpose and point you in the right direction. Invite change into your life and welcome change for your highest good.

I know people who are stuck in their jobs and actually hate them, but they feel they cannot change jobs because of the money, benefits, or security. What I know for sure and see repeatedly is when a person is living their life purpose, everything is provided for them at a deeper and more abundant way than they could have imagined.

You know you are living your life purpose when you step into your work or career with passion and purpose. When each day you are excited about what you have to offer others and the difference you make. When the job is no longer a job. When time flies by. When instead of being drained or tired, you are exhilarated. Gratitude fills your heart and spirit when you are fully present in what you are doing.

Since 1986, I've been living my life purpose, as was given to me from God, in 1984, *"Become a healer, teach around the world, and writes books."* When I do speaking engagements it is as if my ego steps aside and my true essence or Spirit moves and speaks through me. When my presentations are over I feel uplifted, excited, peaceful, joyous, and know I have made a difference.

It doesn't matter what position you hold; if it is your life purpose, you will express and experience it with passion and love. Step into your true self and let your greatness and brilliance shine!

Magic happens if we're open to it. My inspiration to touch people extended farther than I'd dreamed, to the realm of visual arts. Winter 2008, I was Divinely guided to create, and produce a documentary about near-death experiences.

I spoke with my editor of this book, Monica, about it, and she called me back the next day, wanting to help. Our plans for a documentary, *Dying to Live: NDE,* bloomed, and I found assistance showing up from many sources—a seasoned photographer who also specialized in lighting and editing, an accomplished songwriter who created our original theme song, offers to loan us equipment, and advice from other filmmakers.

Plus donations! Offers of assistance! Enthusiasm! Our January filming plans leaped closer and we started taping interviews two months earlier than we expected. The Universe had its own plans, and we are allowing Spirit to move through us.

Manifestations of our dreams are feelings woven within us. What are you waiting for? Express them now! Do what you were born to do!

Make Your Needs Known

I cannot tell you how many times, in the past, I have judged someone because I thought they *(should)* know what I wanted or needed. After all, doesn't everyone read minds? NO! We just think they *should* be able to.

It is extremely important we speak our truth and let our needs and desires be known. It doesn't matter how simple or elaborate—we need to speak up. Many people grew up being taught it was wrong to ask for things, but in reality when you ask, your needs can be met. It doesn't matter if it is support, something material, or something small or large. Whatever your needs, they are real to you and people feel important when they can help.

I remember so many times when someone wanted to help me and I would say, "No that's okay, I can do it myself." The truth was at times I wanted their assistance, but part of me felt powerless if I couldn't do it myself, and I didn't want to take up their precious time. When I learned to allow others to help me, not only did it make it easier for me, but also the person felt like they were giving a gift of service. In addition, when I didn't allow them to help me, I took something away from them. When you begin to identify your needs and express them, it empowers you, and when you share your needs, it allows a connection to another person.

Don't carry the ball and chain around any longer. Let it go! Allow your needs and desires to be known. Let people support you in any way they can. Both of you will truly feel blessed.

Ask and Surrender

Throughout your life there may be things you wanted to obtain, be, or do, but the voices of limitation, lack, and fear in your head say it isn't good to ask for what you want. The only limitation in this world is the limitation of your thoughts. What you think is what is true for you. So if you think you don't deserve the best, you will behave in a way and do what is necessary to make that the case. To change your life and move forth in the abundance that is your birthright as a wonderful, unique, individualized expression of the Divine, you must first change your thinking. In Ernest Holmes teachings he writes, "Change your thinking, change your life."

You are a child of God and abundance in every area of your life is your birthright. Infinite Spirit wants you to have your heart's desire and to be joyous. The first step is to visualize what you want—see it, taste it, smell it, and make it yours in your mind. The more you vividly feel and create in your mind's eye what you want, the stronger the vibration and reality of your goals, dreams, and desires can then come forth into manifestation.

The next step is to move into the silence through meditation or simply follow your breath and ask your heart what it desires right now for your highest good. Listen and you will receive your answer.

Ask, "Am I prepared for this?" Next ask, "What do I need to do to prepare to receive that which I desire?" Listen to the guidance, and take the steps necessary to manifest your dreams.

Now is the time for thanksgiving, knowing through this process you have begun co-creation with Spirit working through you. It is important to remember Divine timing is perfect and isn't necessarily on your timetable, so be patient and believe!

All you have to do is ask, believe, and let go! When you find yourself struggling to make something happen and experience resistance, this is a clue to stop, breathe, and re-vision your path. Co-creation always happens easily and effortlessly. Resistance warns you are on the wrong path. Get out of the way and let it flow to you. Surrender and allow space for your highest good to be revealed and made manifest.

In setting goals, follow these simple steps:

1. Set a goal you are committed to.
2. Be flexible about how to get there.
3. Don't be attached to the goal or how to achieve it.
4. Celebrate.

In *The Illuminated Rumi*, Rumi expresses, "Let yourself be silently drawn by the stronger pull of what you really love."

Esther and Jerry Hicks' book, *Ask and It is Given: Learning to Manifest Your Desires,* will "Assist you in reconnecting with the 'Non-Physical' part of yourself, and in achieving anything you desire." This is a book you can read and re-read many times and still find a new jewel with each reading. It is easy to understand and written so it touches various types of people. There is something for everyone here.

You are never detached from anything. You are always everything, in everything, for everything. You glow within this energy. Embrace all that your heart desires. Open your heart to receive. It is your birthright!

❧ ❧

Secrets and Telling the Truth

When you lie, hold back the truth, or keep secrets, your soul suffers. Your spirit only knows the truth, and when you don't speak it or act upon it, your soul diminishes. In some cases you no longer feel empowered or lively. When you hold back the truth or lie, you disconnect, because you aren't allowing your spirit to be expressed. When you don't speak your truth or act in integrity you experience pain, suffering, and separation.

When my grandfather raped me for nine years I had to keep a deep dark secret. He threatened me with "If you tell anyone, I will kill your Mommy." The only one who heard the truth about my abuse was my baby doll, Susie, my Angel, and Infinite Spirit. My deep-seated anger, hurt, rage, sadness, and confusion led to low self-esteem, blame, shame, and guilt. Years later I was so full of unexpressed emotions I became suicidal and anorexic and was hospitalized for three months. While in the hospital, at the age of 34, I had to admit the truth to my parents about my grandfather raping me, in order for my healing process to begin.

I will never forget how my father responded about his dad raping me. "If he were alive today I would kill him," he said. My heart opened up. That was a validation that if my dad had known, he would have protected me. From that moment on, my relationship with him became stronger and I felt safer than ever before.

Later when I found out my ex-husband was infected with HIV/AIDS, I only told the truth to my sister, my boyfriend, Sid, and my minister. The lie of not sharing my health problems with my parents and daughter interfered with the close relationship we once had. When they asked me what I had been doing, or how I was, I didn't tell them the truth. I didn't want them to worry about me. However, a year later I felt truly blessed when I told them about being infected. They embraced me and supported me in every possible way they could.

Maybe you can relate to this: I remember growing up and having a lot of little unimportant secrets. It was hard to keep track of who I told what. The secrets were eating me away.

It is amazing how uplifting and wonderful it feels when you tell the truth and set secrets free. Once your secrets are out in the open you don't have to hide behind them anymore. I feel more alive and free as I express the truth. It also allows me to connect from the center of my heart with pureness, and honesty. By telling the truth I preserve my integrity. Honor your voice and speak your truth!

A remarkable friend of mine, Stuart Altschuler, is a licensed marriage and family therapist and AM radio talk show host of *Tell the Truth, Faster!* He states:

TELL THE TRUTH, FASTER!

> Withholding an honest expression of our thoughts and feelings can impact our health, relationships, self–esteem, career, and sex life. The more we repress what we need to communicate, whether it is anger or love, the more our bodies have to work overtime to cope with the stress and tension this causes. We all know this can lead to physical problems like headaches, ulcers, fatigue, and immune system weakness. But what many of us don't realize is how withholding our truth can also adversely

impact our relationships and our ability to be intimate. When we fear being "found out" or fear having to deal with another person's reaction to what we say, we build a barrier between them and us. This creates distance within a relationship. We have all learned to fear honesty (as individuals and a society). We need to learn how to change this habit of keeping secrets. People fear change and it takes an honest and courageous individual to make a difference. This is essential to our individual and collective survival. This applies to professional as well as personal relationships.

What kind of world would this be, if no one knew how to lie? How different would personal, professional, and political relationships be if there were no games or manipulation? How do we determine what our own truth is, and how can we learn to communicate what we really want to say without letting fear create our real life soap operas? This is the core of what it means to "Tell the Truth, Faster!"

Our spirit soars when we express ourselves—be it through words, gestures, movement, or clothing. How often do you hold back from expressing yourself because you feel you might be judged?

It is just as important for children to express themselves. However, so many times parents, society, clergy, and teachers don't allow that to happen. If what they express isn't hurting another person or themselves, why not let them be who they are?

It may be a phase they go through, or it may be part of them that will remain throughout their lives.

In the early 1990s, Jeaneen attended the Visual Arts Magnet Program at Fairfax High School in Hollywood, California. She expressed herself through dance, music, and photography.

Every morning I looked forward to how Jeaneen was going to reveal herself. Sometimes she had purple, pink, or green hair. She wore Goth clothing and make up. I loved it!

She and her friends were creative and made a lot of their own outfits. On weekends I would take them to dance clubs and they would all be dressed up in black attire, wild hair, and jet black make-up.

Some people thought because of the way they dressed they were probably troublemakers. Believe me, these girls and boys had more compassion and love than most kids their age because they had freedom to express themselves.

As long as children aren't harming another or themselves, allow them to express who they truly are.

When was the last time you expressed who you truly are? That is part of Telling the Truth. Let yourself shine brightly!

Gratitude

Gratitude has many meanings such as thankfulness, thanks, gratefulness, appreciation, acknowledgement, recognition, and thanksgiving.

Most of us have more blessings than we can count in a given day. These can include home, friends and loved ones, freedom, jobs, transportation, religious facility, food, water, and clothing. What about the parts of you that you take for granted: your heart, life force, your eyes, feet, and hands. Be grateful for the beauty upon Mother Earth: the trees, lush plants, green rolling hills, mighty mountain ranges, beautiful ocean, and the tame and wild animals. Be thankful for the enjoyment of seeing a magnificent sunrise or sunset in all its glorious colors, the sound of a baby cooing, the sound of the wind in the mighty trees, the sound of the birds singing outside your window, the sound of chimes as they blow in the wind, the sound of powerful waves crashing on the shore, or the sound of someone saying "I love you."

Give gratitude for your pets. For some people these are their children. Pets bring comfort, love, affection, and devotion.

When you sit down and think about gratitude, think about how fortunate you are compared to millions of other men, women, and children throughout the world who have no shelter or clothing and are dying from abuse, thirst, hunger, and from *disease*.

Begin to notice your blessings. I write in a gratitude journal all of my daily blessings. When I feel discouraged, I read through my journal and recall in my mind and heart all the wonderful things and people I am truly grateful for.

Sarah Ban Breathnach is the author of a series of books on *Simple Abundance*. Her books are meaningful and I use her *Simple Abundance Journal of Gratitude*.

When you are sincerely grateful, your heart is open, and acts of kindness stimulate the body's immune system and give a greater sense of inner peace and centeredness.

Here are a few simple examples of how to show gratitude:

1. Say "thank you" as often as you can—to the bank teller, the grocer, the postman, your children, Mother Earth and all of her surroundings, and the sacred parts of your body.

2. Handwrite a thank you note when you receive a gift or appreciate something someone has done for you.

3. Surprise someone with something special.

4. Show your emotions through a smile, gesture, hug, kiss, or facial expression.

5. When you write a check to someone, write, "I Gratefully" above their name. It would read, "I gratefully pay to the order of (their name)."

6. On your checks above your signature write, "Thank You." When you open your heart to doing number 5 and 6 on your checks it is amazing how magical it feels to pay your bills or purchase things.

7. Open the door in public for strangers.

8. Donate time or money to your favorite organization or charity.

9. From time to time throughout the day, give thanks for your life and well-being.

10. Give compliments.

11. Consciously listen to what people say.

12. Take time for yourself and honor who you are.

13. Give a hug—studies show that babies who are held often are healthier and grow faster, compared to those who aren't held as much. Human contact is necessary for life. How many hugs did you give or receive today?

14. Give gratitude for your meals (prayer).

15. Be a regular blood donor.

16. Plant a tree or help restore the environment.

17. Conserve water and electricity.

18. Recycle.

19. Be thankful for medications (Holistic and Western). I wish I didn't have to take Western medications, but from time to time, my body needs them. When it does, I thank my body for letting me know. When I receive my medications, I place them in my hands and give thanks to my doctor and my body for knowing what I need, the scientist that discovered the remedy, the FDA for its approval, and the pharmacy personnel who filled my

prescription with love. I also give thanks for each pill, knowing it will nurture my body, mind, and spirit in a positive and uplifting way. I give thanks for the perfect results that come from the medications.

20. Give thanks for your heartbeat and your breath of life.

The energy of gratitude is expansive and assists you to connect with your Spirit. Start making a list of ALL you are thankful for. Don't just write them down, feel the emotion and energy as you write what you are grateful for. Let the feeling of gratitude fill your heart and mind. Each day add something new to your list. It is amazing how uplifted you will feel as you acknowledge your blessings. Your heart will open wide.

I remember one evening when I visited an amazing man, Dr. John Demartini, concerning his endorsement for my first book, *Sacred Living, Sacred Dying: A Guide to Embracing Life and Death.* As we shared stories he mentioned if every person would write at least 1,000 things they were thankful for, the world around us would rapidly change. How long is your list?

Below are a few beautiful quotations about gratitude:

- ❖ "Blessed are those that can give without remembering and receive without forgetting." ~ Author Unknown

- ❖ "He is a wise man who does not grieve for the things which he has not, but rejoices for those which he has." ~ Epictetus

- ❖ "If the only prayer you ever say in your life is thank you, it will be enough." ~ Author Unknown

❖ "There is a common element in the ability to see beauty, appreciate simple things, to enjoy your own company or to relate to other people with loving kindness. This common element is a sense of contentment, peace, and aliveness that is the invisible background without which these experiences would not be possible. This is the Sweetness of Being." ~ Eckhart Tolle, *The New Earth: Awakening to Your Life's Purpose.*

It is important to show gratitude for good things, but it is just as important to acknowledge your so-called negative experiences or challenges:

❖ Be thankful for all your challenges. They give you an opportunity to grow and be true to yourself.

❖ Be thankful for the job you lost. Now you can create new opportunities for yourself.

❖ Be thankful for lost relationships. They allowed you to experience and grow in areas of your life.

❖ Be thankful for your mistakes. They teach you valuable lessons.

Dr. John F. Demartini states in, *Count Your Blessings: The Healing Power of Gratitude and Love,* "The people who irritate us the most are the ones we might want to observe the most. They're reflecting back to us those things about ourselves that we haven't learned to feel grateful for and love. Since our mission is to discover what we don't love and learn to love it, the people who get on our nerves most are among our greatest teachers!"

As you give thanks for your challenges and open your eyes and heart to the blessings that lie within, this is when healing and growth can really begin. Part of our life journey is to discover the positive within the so-called negative.

At the end of the evening when I fall into a space of tranquility, I reflect upon the happenings of the day and give thanks for all that has been brought into my life. Know everything is in Divine and perfect order right now. Give gratitude for this moment!

Forgiveness

At what point do you forgive another? For me forgiveness didn't always happen immediately. Sometimes it didn't happen until the non-forgiveness was destroying me, to the point of death. By not forgiving my grandfather for raping me and my ex-husband for his abuse, I gave away my power to them. My thoughts were consumed with negativity. I lost all sense of inner peace and began a war within my own mind, body, and spirit. It was so bad I ended up sick.

On television there are stories about mothers who forgave the drunk drivers who killed their children, or the parents who forgave the man, woman, or adolescent who murdered their child. Through their forgiveness, their hearts expanded to greater love and they may have become involved with organizations concerned with the problem, such as a mother working with the MADD Program—Mothers Against Drunk Driving.

Colin C. Tipping's book *Radical Forgiveness: Making Room for the Miracles* helps guide us to understand and pursue forgiveness. I wish I had his book while I was going through my healing process, but it hadn't been published yet. Colin's information is extremely valuable, and the Radical Forgiveness Worksheet and Release Letter can easily assist you in forgiveness.

How did I learn to forgive?

- ❖ First and most important, I realized I could be a victim, or I could make a conscious choice to learn the lessons and allow the experiences to empower me. The choice was mine.

❖ I didn't deny or minimize the hurt. I felt the hurt and experienced it, but I didn't continue to allow the hurt to control me.

❖ I had to realize I couldn't change the past, but I could change the present.

❖ I wrote letters to my grandfather. Since he was dead, I burned them in a ceremony. If he had been alive, I would have mailed the letters to him. In my letters I wrote the feelings of anger, resentment, disgust, humiliation, shame, and the betrayal I felt due to his actions and behaviors. I wrote how much I suffered losing my innocence at such a young age and how I had grown up faster than I was supposed to.

❖ I wrote letters to my ex–husband, Bill, and told him how betrayed and hurt I felt for his action and behaviors. Then I realized Bill in some ways hurt as much as I did. I needed to feel what I felt, but I also needed to forgive him. I called upon his Spirit and dialogued with him until there was peace between us.

❖ I did every process and exercise in this book—body dialogue, visualizations, emotional clearing, chair-to-chair communication, affirmations, yelling into pillows, making clay models and destroying them, cutting the cords (found in the next sub-chapter), and completing sentence stems. Sometimes I did the processes repeatedly before I felt inner peace, freedom, and heartfelt forgiveness. Each step of the way was rewarding and insightful.

❖ I realized my grandfather and my ex-husband didn't know how to express love in a positive way. I am not the one to judge them. My life has been full of lessons because of their actions and behaviors that on some level I agreed to participate in. I have become a better person because of what they taught me. I forgive them and I bless them for helping me discover my authentic self through my life challenges with them.

❖ I took responsibility for how I felt and wrote my emotions, feelings, and thoughts on paper. Sometimes I would burn them and release them in a ceremony.

❖ I prayed for forgiveness, not only for others but also for myself, to find compassion and understanding.

❖ I knew as long as I didn't forgive, the other person had a hold on my life and well-being. That is no longer the case. I am my own creator. I have learned to accept others as they are, knowing like me they are an expression of Infinite Spirit. As I embraced others, love allowed me to see the Sacred Beings they are.

❖ Throughout my life I have learned to forgive myself for the actions, thoughts, and behaviors I have placed upon others and myself—including decades ago when I cheated on my husband.

❖ I realized problems with a person or situation mirrored a part of me that was not connected to my wholeness.

❖ I learned to understand every experience brought me into greater alignment with the truth of who I am.

❖ As I forgive others, I am offered understanding where previously there was none. When I affirm, "I care about you and about our relationship," I give another and myself a chance to make the connection better between us.

❖ Through the dark periods of my life I was able to awaken to the Divinity within.

❖ I learned our greatest rewards always lie on the other side of our greatest challenges.

❖ Through forgiveness I was able to reclaim my power and dignity.

❖ I chose to see the Divinity in the person, rather than hold onto the circumstances.

❖ I realized forgiveness is for me and no one else.

❖ I recognized judgment creates separation.

❖ I learned out of conflict comes courage.

❖ Within my heart I needed to find peace.

❖ We are all a spark of God.

❖ We are all Beings of love, connected to the Oneness of All. How could I not forgive?

❖ Forgiveness heals.

❖ Love heals!

A Course in Miracles says, "All *dis-ease* comes from a state of unforgiveness," and "whenever we are ill, we need to look around to see who it is that we need to forgive."

Louise L. Hay adds to that concept in her book *You Can Heal Your Life,* when she states, "The very person you find it hardest to forgive is the one YOU NEED TO LET GO OF THE MOST."

The Buddha said, "Hatred never ceases by hatred, but by love alone is healed." This is the ancient and eternal law.

In Stephen Levine's book, *Unattended Sorrows*, he writes, "Healing is entering, with mercy and awareness, into those areas of ourselves we have withdrawn from with fear and a sense of helplessness. Healing is reoccupying those parts of ourselves that we abandoned because of mental or physical pain. Healing is replacing our merciless reactions with a merciful response. Without mercy, we don't have a chance. And that chance is the breadth of heart that is our birthright."

Below is a forgiveness process I do:

❖ I see myself standing on an arched bridge and beneath me runs clear water. I see, envision, imagine, and sense the person I want to ask forgiveness from, or I need to forgive, come before me on the bridge.

This person appears as a baby with the face (like an adult, adolescent, or child) of the person I know. The baby is bundled up in a blanket. I place the baby in my arms. As I look at the baby, I recognize them and say whatever I need to until I feel complete. Then I say to the baby, "I ask for your forgiveness for whatever I may have done or said, intentionally or unintentionally, that caused you pain and suffering. I ask that you forgive me."

Then I say, "I forgive you for whatever you may have done or said intentionally or unintentionally that caused me pain and suffering. I forgive you from the center of my heart."

Then I wrap a cord around the baby's waist area and slowly lower the baby into the water. As I lower the baby into the water I say, "I set you free and I ask you to set me free." As the baby floats in the slow, moving current, I watch the current take the baby out of my vision.

During the final weeks of Bill's life he called me while I was out of town. He left a message that he needed to speak to me. When I returned he had already died from AIDS complications. I truly believe in my heart Bill called to ask for my forgiveness. I had forgiven him already, but I connected with his spirit and sent him love. I knew in my heart Bill never intended to infect me with HIV/AIDS, and his verbal and emotional abuse is what he experienced as a child.

It is never too late to forgive. My suggestion to you is do whatever it takes to forgive another and yourself, so you may live in peace and truly embrace life and humanity.

❧   ☙

Cutting the Cords

Throughout our lives we come across relationships that need to be severed for one reason or another. As you go your separate ways, you may still feel a tug or pull toward that person, yet you know it is for your highest good to let them go. I have experienced using the cord-cutting process to be extremely healing for me and the other person. There is no blame, guilt, or shame, only love.

Below is the process I use:

1. Find a comfortable position where you feel relaxed.

2. Gently close your eyes.

3. Take a couple slow deep breaths in through your nose and exhale through your mouth.

4. Imagine, visualize, or sense the person standing before you.

5. State their name and thank them for coming to you.

6. Say, "I care about you and about your well-being. I thank you for coming into my life and for the lessons I have learned. Now it is time for me to release you and I ask that you also release me."

7. Feel or perhaps even see where energy cords connect you to the other person. You can pass your hand down the

front side of your body and feel a shift of energy where the cords are attached. It may be in the heart area, solar plexus, head, or somewhere else. It doesn't matter. Just notice how many cords and where they are located.

8. Now see yourself with a laser beam, scissors, or any cutting instrument that seems appropriate to you.

9. State something that feels comfortable, such as, "As I cut these cords from you, I release you to all that is for your highest good and I ask you to release me to all that is for my highest good. I set you free and ask that you set me free."

10. Then cut the cords.

11. Say, "Thank you for my freedom and I set you free."

12. Now imagine, sense, or see the person vanish.

13. As the cords hang outside your body, begin to pull them out.

14. When the ends of the cords are removed from your body, place your hands on the areas where you pulled out the cords and fill the areas with loving energy.

15. Notice how peaceful you feel.

16. Take a deep breath in through your nose and exhale through your mouth. When you feel comfortable, gently open your eyes.

This is a powerful clearing of heart, mind, and spirit as you release someone into their highest good.

Hugs

Hug friends, loved ones, or strangers heart to heart. As adults we protect our hearts by not letting people close. Yet, most people, when they hug a baby or child, hug them heart to heart. Let us get back to the connection and be conscious of how we hug people.

If you do muscle testing, you will discover many times when you hug a person right shoulder to right shoulder, you become weak. The heart is located at the center of your chest, yet when you hug a person left shoulder to left shoulder, your energy remains strong – heart to heart.

Some cultures and people are offended or don't like to be hugged. If you want to hug a person you don't know well, first ask for permission and then respect their decision.

Research shows hugs are healing and lift your spirit. When was the last time you gave or received a hug? Remember heart to heart.

Intimate Relationships

It is hard to believe I could write about intimate relationships. Believe me I am no expert!

I have had several unsuccessful marriages. My first marriage was in 1969 at the age of 19 to Tom, a talented, professional drummer. He was a loving man whom I loved but didn't know how to love because I was emotionally paralyzed from my sexual abuse. Tom and I divorced and remarried again in 1972. In 1975, we were blessed to give birth to our precious, beautiful daughter Jeaneen. In 1978, Tom and I divorced again.

My next marriage was in 1983 to Bill, a man I thought was Prince Charming until the day of our wedding. During the six months of our marriage, his emotional and mental abuse ripped me apart to the point where I became anorexic and suicidal. I attempted suicide twice, and was given my life purpose—to become a healer, teach around the world, and write books.

Then I married a soft spoken, wise, gentle, spiritual man by the name of Sid, now known as Michael. He was a healer and instrumental in my spiritual growth and health. However, after four years together, our paths went in different directions. I feel blessed because Michael and I still keep in contact.

I have learned a lot from what I have gone through, and I would like to share this with you.

❖ Be true to your core values and yourself at all times. Make a list of your core values such as honor, love, honesty, playfulness, trust, and so forth. Then notice your top four core values. Mine are love, spirituality, integrity, and service, while someone else's might be humor, wealth, family, and intimacy. Everyone has core values.

Then make a list of 50 or more things you would want in your intimate relationship. Be specific. I made a list of my core values and then a list of 50 things I wanted in my next intimate relationship. A lot of my core values were included. One important item on my list was that he respects his mother or sister if he had one, because if he respected them, he would respect me. Also, I didn't want a "Momma's Boy."

When you get to know a person and learn their core values, you will get a good sense if it is a relationship worth your time and energy.

I wrote my list of what I was looking for in a relationship and read it in the morning and evening for a while. Then I put it away and forgot about it. A year later Hector came into my life. Now as I review my list, Hector matched all but one item. The one he didn't match we work on together.

I have suggested this exercise to a lot of my friends, and it is fabulous to witness how they end up attracting that which they truly desire and is for their highest good.

If you have been in a good relationship but it didn't work out, take the good qualities of the person, and then add in the qualities that were missing. Look at the so-called negative aspect of them you didn't like and turn it around to the positive and add it to your list. As an example: If they were messy and that disturbed you, put on your list, they are neat and organized.

In Dr. John F. Demartini's book *The Heart of Love: How to Go Beyond Fantasy to Find True Relationship Fulfillment* he states, "Your values will tend to express themselves in some or all of seven areas of life: spiritual, mental, vocational, financial, familial, social, and physical." His book assists you to understand core values and true relationships.

❖ If a man or woman is abusive to you once and tells you they will never do it again, don't believe it.

I was in two abusive relationships, one physical and one extremely emotional and mental. Their abuse ripped me apart, but I allowed it because I stayed in the relationships.

Once your partner has been abusive with you, the abuse will show up again from time to time—sometimes sooner than later. Walk away from the relationship, even if you need to find support from a therapist, friend, clergy, or the courts. Abuse is not love. Sometimes you may think there will never be another person out there for you, so why not put up with the abuse. Believe me, living alone in peace is much more fulfilling than living in abuse.

Plus, by walking away you are giving the abuser a chance to see the truth—and an opportunity to change who they are in relationship to how they view themselves, and others.

❖ Don't think you will change a person. You need to accept them as they are now. You can only change yourself. If you don't like the person you are with, first think about what attracted you to them. Then look at what is bothering you, and what or how *you* need to change.

- ❖ Don't lose your identity. Over and over I have seen myself lost in a relationship. Once I was in the relationship, I stopped doing what I enjoyed, stopped visiting my friends, and everything revolved around him.

- ❖ Be honest, sincere, clear, and share who you are without pretense.

- ❖ Take responsibility in your relationship. Don't blame the other person.

- ❖ Communicate, communicate, communicate. Speak from your heart.

- ❖ Don't be controlling or have a hidden agenda.

- ❖ Set boundaries.

- ❖ Listen to each other's needs beneath the words.

- ❖ Be a source of support and empowerment.

- ❖ Never go to bed angry.

- ❖ Show respect.

I met the love of my life, Hector, in 2000 when I was not looking for a relationship. I was happy the way my life was going and didn't want to complicate it. However, my life changed forever when I walked into the copy center Hector managed. The moment our eyes met, we knew there was something special. Yet, his energy was so intense I was afraid to pursue it.

Hector's appearance and energy come across as Incan, Hawaiian Shaman, or Native American Healer, yet he is Mexican. He stands 5'10", but you would assume he stands 6'3'' tall. His broad shoulders make me feel protected. His smooth, milky chocolate skin shines healthy and vibrant. His dark brown eyes come alive with light. His black and gray mustache outlines his beautiful upper lip and warm, loving smile. His jet black hair covers up his few silver hairs. When I first saw Hector, he looked like a painting I have of an Inca warrior I purchased in Peru.

Every time I went into Hector's store he would ask me out, and I would say no. I was happy with every aspect of my life, and I wasn't interested in getting into a relationship, so why would I go out?

About a month after meeting Hector, three of my friends—surprisingly their names are Carol, Carole, and Sharon—from Las Vegas came to visit me. They met Hector and told me to go out with him. But I chose not to.

Carol told my dad about Hector, and within a few months my dad came to visit me. My dad decided to check out Hector, without letting him know who he was. As my dad entered the store, Hector greeted him with a smile and said, "Good Morning Sir." My dad was impressed by how he was greeted.

Then my dad said he wanted to make a copy and proceeded to go toward the copy machine. Hector said, "Please allow me to make your copy." My dad thought that was nice of him.

After making the copy my dad asked, "How much do I owe you?"

Hector's response was, "Nothing sir. Have a great day and God Bless You." Needless to say, my dad was sold on Hector, and Hector had no idea who my dad was.

When my dad came home he said, "Go out with this guy."

The next day I went into the store, and Hector once again invited me out. This time I agreed. That weekend when he came over to my house to pick me up for dinner, I told him before we went out I needed to tell him something about my life.

Hector said he didn't want to know anything about my past because it didn't matter. All that mattered was he found me.

I told him if he didn't let me tell him about my past I wouldn't go out with him. For the next half hour we went back and forth. Finally he agreed to sit down and listen.

As I looked into his deep brown loving eyes, I told him I was infected with AIDS and how I became infected.

His response was, "So, that doesn't change how I feel about you." Then he went on to say, "I need to tell you something too." My mind was racing. What was he going to tell me?

Hector held my hand, looked deep into my hazel eyes, and with all sincerity said, "I have been married twice."

I lowered my head, with a smile on my face, and said, "I have been married four times—twice to the same man."

We both laughed.

Hector became more educated about HIV/AIDS, and fear never entered his mind or heart. We have been together ever since. The only hard times we had were at the beginning when I fought off his love for me and didn't allow it in. My therapist, Gita Morena, assisted me to open up my heart more fully to receive Hector's immense love, compassion, intimacy, and devotion. He has assisted me to awaken and love all aspects of myself.

Hector stopped managing the copy center shortly after we met. He said he only worked there to meet me again. He is now living his life purpose, full-time, as an amazing *Divine Spiritual Healer*. Hector was born with the gift of healing and even as a child he knew his gift. He heals people all over the world, in person and over the phone.

It is a blessing from Infinite Spirit that Hector and I are now living our life purpose, and that we found one another! We are two complete whole souls walking side by side in all that we do, in love!

Communicating with the Kingdoms

Throughout *The Integrated Being* I have talked about the different kingdoms, such as plant, mineral, animal, human, and spirit. All kingdoms have their own consciousness and when we quiet the chatter in our minds we can become attuned to the various kingdoms and consciously become one with them. My life wouldn't be complete if I didn't realize I was connected to the various kingdoms and their ways.

One of the greatest lessons I have learned is the only thing separating me from anything is myself.

When Jeaneen was a child and adolescent, on her birthdays we would celebrate the day of her birth, as well as the entire birthday year. We would invite her friends (4-6 girls) over for a slumber party. I loved to hear the girl's giggle, watch them play, and join in on their games. Even though it was Jeaneen's birthday, everyone received gifts.

One activity the girls looked forward to, year after year, was visualizations to get in touch with their Angels or Spirit Guides.

I had the girls lie on the floor and I talked them through the visualization, which is outlined in the sub-chapter "Angels, Archangels, and Spirit Guides." Each one met a Celestial Being and was given loving messages. To this day some of Jeaneen's friends still feel connected to their Angel and Spirit Guides and talk to them on a regular basis.

I also had a large bouquet of assorted flowers and each girl picked out a flower. Then I had them hold their flower and really look at it—from the top, bottom, and sides. I asked them to smell the fragrance, and then gently close their eyes while they held their flower.

1. I told them, "Thank your flower for getting your attention."

2. I asked them, "What does your flower want to tell you?"

    They listened and heard.

3. "Why were you drawn to this flower?"

    They listened.

4. "How does this flower represent a part of you?"

    They heard, and had smiles on their faces.

5. "Now ask your flower any questions you may have."

    They asked and listened.

6. "Is there anything else this flower wants to tell you?"

    They listened and some heard more.

7. Then I gave instructions to, "Thank your flower for the messages you received and for the beautiful gift of life it gave up for you to enjoy its essence."

8. Then I had them open their eyes and allowed them share their experiences and messages they received.

Sometimes I would take the girls outside and find a flower in the garden. Instead of picking the flower, they would hold their hands around the stem and really look at the flower. Then I talked them through the same process. I remember one time Jeaneen's friend, Lynette, walked over to a flower growing close to my house and after her conversation with the flower, she came up to me and said, "Sharon, this flower wants to be moved because it isn't getting enough sunlight and it wants a lot more." HMMM. Listen!

Below is an easy example of how you can become aware of, communicate with, and work with the various kingdoms:

1. Find a comfortable place where you can let go of the outside world and become calm and relaxed.

2. Gently close your eyes.

3. Take a couple of deep slow breaths, in through your nose and out through your mouth. Now state, "At this time I set aside my fear and my ego to experience the truth of:

   a. the Spirit of _____ (the person, animal…..)

   b. the Spirit energy of this _____ (crystal, planet, ……)

   c. my Angel _____)

4. Once you have called them forth, you want to acknowledge their presence.

   a. Thank you _____ for coming to me, or

   b. Thank you _____ for appearing before me.

5. Ask the crystal, spirit guide, plant, or any other kingdom any of these questions that may apply:

    a. What do you want to tell me at this time?

    b. What do you want to show me?

    c. What do I need to know about _____?

    d. What do you want to tell me concerning _____?

    e. What do you want to show me regarding _____?

    f. Now take time to ask whatever you want.

6. When you feel complete, give thanks and then ask one last time, "Is there anything else I need to know at this time?"

7. Always give thanks for the crystal, spirit guide, angel, animal, or plant kingdom for connecting with you.

8. Take a deep breath in and slowly release it. Begin to notice the sounds around you. Take your time, and when you feel comfortable slowly open your eyes.

❖ You can also call in your friends and allies such as money, confidence, strength, or wisdom and have them work with you.

    a. Courage I need you. Courage I need more of you. Courage I need your help. Courage I need your assistance.

b. Be specific. I want or need (courage, money, confidence, strength, wisdom) to come to me quickly under grace and in perfect ways.

c. When or if you sense fear, take a moment to say, "Thank you fear for being my friend, but I don't need you at this time. Please stand aside and let (courage, wisdom . . .) be with me or work with me at this time. Fear, I will call you when I need you. Thank you."

d. Thank you (courage, wisdom. . .) for coming to me and working with me. I look forward to calling upon you again soon.

e. Friends or Allies, thank you for supporting me and all my needs and desires.

f. At this time I accept all that is for my highest good and all that is for the highest good of all concerned.

g. Take a deep breath in and slowly release it. Begin to notice the sounds around you. Take your time, and when you feel comfortable slowly open your eyes.

Enjoy connecting to the various kingdoms. Call upon them. They are waiting to assist you!

ॐ   ॐ

Going Within

From time to time I find it extremely helpful to take time away from everything and everyone, to go within and seek guidance, renewal, and solitude. I have found not only meditation, but also silence retreats, sweat lodges, and vision quests offer an amazing, peaceful, connected, and harmonious feeling.

I have attended three-day silent retreats at local monasteries. The monks or nuns provide participants with their own room, nutritious meals, and if you choose you can join them for meditation. Nothing disturbs you except your own thoughts. Silence is a time to focus within. There is no television, radio, reading, or distraction. The only distraction is the chatter of your mind which before long will be silent. You are with your mind, your heart, and nature. You eat in silence, walk in silence, and don't make eye contact with anyone. You are absorbed within your own Being and surroundings. Your thoughts may first be around fear, because you have lost all connection to what is familiar. Once the inner chatter softens, the voice of the heart through Spirit speaks and sings. The voice of love, respect, honor, compassion, unity, devotion, inner peace, and stillness becomes a powerful force. This is a force that lives deep within for a long time after a silence retreat.

If you find it difficult to get away for a three-day silent retreat, think about being silent for a day. It may take some time to get to the center of your Being and embrace the silence, but it is worth it. Allow yourself the opportunity to go deep within to the silence of your Being.

Labyrinth

Another method I have used to go within is through a labyrinth walk. I have walked many labyrinths which led me to the center of my Being and back again into the world. In my sacred walk I seek Divine Guidance.

What is a labyrinth? It is an ancient symbol that relates to wholeness. It is a metaphor for life's journey. It is different than a maze which has twists, turns, and blind alleys. Instead, a labyrinth has only one path that leads you to the center. The way in is the way out.

There are various indoor and outdoor types of labyrinths. I have walked ones made from stones/rocks, plants, small bushes, and canvas. Recently I noticed more churches have set up canvas labyrinths for their congregation members.

The walk into, through, and out is a sacred walk and can be used as a meditation or prayer tool. From time to time I have consciously brought my attitude into a state of joyfulness, thoughtfulness, gratitude, sorrow, or allowed whatever emotion I was experiencing at the time to come forth.

I have walked the labyrinth with groups of people and also individually. I prefer to walk it alone so I can be mindful of each step and breath, so I can be focused on whatever I am bringing into the center.

I approach the labyrinth as a sacred ceremony by the following:

1. Before I go to the ceremony, I decide what issue I want to work on, what question I have, what problems may need to be addressed, or I go in peace and allow whatever I need be revealed when I unite with the center.

2. I decide in advance what special gift I want to present or leave in the center. I have offered crystals, flowers, a rock, a balloon, and sage.

3. As I stand at the start of the labyrinth with my gift in hand, I pause, become quiet and centered. I give thanks and show gratitude by getting on my knees and bowing my head down to the ground.

4. As I enter, I walk purposefully, and when I reach the center I stay there as long as I feel drawn to do so. When I am in the center, sometimes I sit, lie down, or stand. I have stayed in the middle of the labyrinth as long as 30 minutes, but usually once I arrive in the center, within five minutes I receive my message or answer.

5. After I feel complete, I will leave my gift in the center and then turn around and begin my sacred journey out.

6. When I reach the end, I turn and face the entrance. I give thanks and show gratitude for this sacred ceremony by placing my hands in prayer position and bowing my head.

7. After my walk, I allow time to reflect on my labyrinth journey and journal about my experience.

Even though I use the word "walk," I have witnessed people skipping through the labyrinth. Do whatever feels comfortable to you. If you haven't had an opportunity to walk a labyrinth, I know you will feel peaceful and blessed whenever you do.

ल ल

Embracing Native Traditions

Since I was a little girl, I have felt a deep inner connection within my soul and spirit toward the Native American Indian, Mayan, and Inca people, cultures, traditions, history, and ceremonies. Perhaps what has made the native traditions so important in my life is my angel, who taught the ways of native people. I feel a connection to all the kingdoms and can easily communicate with them. I also embrace the native sacred rituals and ceremonies, and incorporate them in different parts of my life:

❖ Sweat Lodges—For centuries Native Americans have entered into the sacred Temescal, or sweat lodge, for purification of mind, body, and spirit. The lodge is built of 16 willow branches fashioned into a framework, which is covered with rugs, tarps, or blankets to contain heat. The sweat lodge is considered the womb of the Mother Earth, and the person reemerges from the lodge reborn into the world.

Since 1986, I have participated in numerous Native American Sweat Lodges as part of my healing process. I find it beneficial to fast or stay on a liquid cleanse the day before I go into the lodge. This is a sacred day of preparation for the sweat and a day of contemplation.

The day of the lodge, I find it important to participate or be present for all aspects of the sweat lodge: gathering wood or sage, (always asking permission to pick the sage), witnessing the fire tenders building the sacred fire, preparing the sweat lodge for the sacred ceremony, and drumming and chanting ancient songs.

Once the rocks (stone people) have been heated in the sacred fire (which usually takes a few hours to turn red hot), participants are smudged/purified with sage or cedar. At the doorway, we call to our relations and ancestors to share in the ceremony with us. We kneel down, bow our heads, and kiss Mother Earth. We acknowledge her for re-birthing us. Until we are born we cannot walk. Then we crawl into the womb (sweat lodge) in a clockwise direction.

After all the participants gather inside, the stones are brought in and gently placed in the pit. Each stone is sprinkled with cedar. After the sacred stones have been sprinkled, the fire tender passes a bucket of water and ladle to the ceremonial leader. The water has been prayed upon and turned into medicine. As part of the blessing, the water (medicine) touches the sacred stones. Then the ceremonial leader instructs the helpers outside the sweat lodge to close the flap (door).

Within the womb it is pitch black. The ceremonial leader will pour water onto the heated stones four times, to honor the four directions. The rocks sizzle and pop, sending up a cloud of steam that fills the lodge. During each round in the sweat lodges I have been in, there is a guided prayer, songs, chanting, and sometimes drumming or silence. We usually have four rounds. When each round is complete, the flap of the door is lifted, and the fire tender places more stone people inside the pit, which increases the temperature, as does the sacred splashing of water on the rocks.

While inside the sweat lodge our sweat, prayers, and chants cleanse our bodies of toxins, release our minds of negative thoughts and beliefs, and heighten our spirits. Sweating creates spiritual cleanliness, and the sweat lodge is a sacred ceremony. The purification also brings into balance our relation-ships with Mother Earth, ourselves, and everything and everyone that surround us.

The community I belong to (Rainbow, with teachings of the Lakota) has sweat lodges once a month. In our sweat lodge, in the first round we give thanks for all our blessings. During the second round we send prayers to other people and situations. In the third round, which seems to be the hottest, we release negative things from our lives that no longer serve us, or aren't for our highest good. The final round manifests a new reality and embraces the sacredness of all. There is always silence after Indian chants or prayers.

After our sweat lodge we take cold showers and dress in fresh clothes. Then we gather to share food and friend-ship.

If you are interested in doing a sacred sweat lodge, there are "hard sweats" and "gentle sweats," depending on the need. Traditions must be followed which are outlined by the tribe preparing the ceremony, such as no one under the influence of drugs or alcohol within 24 hours preceding the ceremony can enter the ceremonial area or the sweat lodge. You may or may not need to be clothed. Women who are menstruating (Moontime) do not enter the sweat lodge with men (however, some tribes allow it). Usually there will be a lodge specifically for women and Moontime. The ceremonial site must be left clean and natural. It is important to approach the ceremonial leader or a knowledgeable staff member prior to entering any ceremony if you have any questions.

Native people by tradition always give an offering before they take anything for their needs. Thus to honor and respect their traditions, a donation or gift is given to the fire tenders and ceremonial leader.

❖ I experienced my first Vision Quest in 1986, with Joan Halifax and Ralph Blum (author of *The Book of Runes*) in the Yucatan. I was drawn to the teaching of the Mayans and the deep need to connect with nature and seek answers from Infinite Spirit. The vision quest was the perfect opportunity to reconnect and listen to God.

We had numerous ceremonies throughout our week-long vision quest in and among the ancient pyramids, the crystal clear ocean, and on sacred grounds. We walked in Mindful Meditation, where we were aware of the placement of our feet upon Mother Earth and gave thanks and gratitude for each step.

We were given several choices as to private two–day visions, and one of my choices was to face the fear of darkness. I agreed to stay in a deep dark cave for two days. My sacred space only extended out three feet in each direction from my body with sage surrounding the border. I could only step out from my sacred place when I had to go to the bathroom. I pushed myself to stay awake the entire time. I drank water, prayed, listened intensely, chanted, and played my drum. I faced my demons and fears, including a snake.

Our next quest was a 24-hour walk on the breathtaking white sandy beach. We were allowed a bottle of water, but it was recommended that, to experience the greatest awareness, we were not to sleep.

As I sought the truth through vision quests, my prayers were answered. I felt a deeper connection to Infinite Spirit and the entire Universe and its elements. I also discovered a profound meaning and direction to my life.

❖ In March 1999, I went on a sacred journey to Peru, lead by Dr. Sharon Forrest. I embraced the sacredness of Inca teachings, traditions, and ceremonies, and learned more about my Spiritual Teacher, Vira Cocha. It took two months to prepare for this quest because of the altitude in Cusco. Vira Cocha assured me I would be fine. I took a lot of antioxidants and visualized myself strong and healthy enough to partake in all of the activities. Our shaman guides warned us that, because of the altitude, we would likely feel sick and have to take some herbs. Thanks to the way I prepared and the blessings of Vira Cocha, I never felt sick. We visited the sacred sites of Lima, Cusco, Saqsaywaman, Moray, Urubama Sacred Valley of the Incas, Ollantaytambu, and Machu Picchu. In each sacred site we performed a ritual, blessing, or ceremony.

As I walked the streets of Peru I was amazed at the beauty of the Inca people, city temples, sacred fortresses, buildings, traditions, ceremonies, and the history. I felt honored to pay homage to the people and the land of Peru and to learn more about the ways and life of Vira Cocha.

My spiritual journey to Peru was a special gift from my mom when she died. She knew the connection I had to all native tribes, and especially to Peru. Throughout my time in Peru, I felt my mom's presence.

❖ In 2003, I had been sick for three months. It wasn't AIDS related, but the doctors and tests couldn't pinpoint what was causing my severe diarrhea. I knew the answer to my health issues was to reconnect with the oneness of all and surrender to Infinite Spirit. I offered tobacco to Happy Bear, a Lakota elder and asked him to put me on a hill for a three-day vision quest, called "Cry for Vision," with no food or water.

Because of my health condition, he told me he wouldn't put me on the hill. The next day during his prayers he asked Great Spirit about me, and he was told to honor my request. When the elder called and invited me to participate in the vision quest, I was thrilled and my spirit lifted. The elder told me I had to remain on my medication and he would silently come to my sacred site and offer me two tablespoons of water and a square inch slice of break twice a day to take with my medications. I also agreed to remain within my sacred circle throughout the vision quest, unless I needed to go to the bathroom in the bushes.

I knew basically it would be three days without food or water. So I called my spiritual friends and asked them to be conscious of the water they drank and every bite of food they ate, while I was on my quest. I asked them to offer some of what they would drink and eat to my spirit. If they did this, I knew I wouldn't be hungry or thirsty.

A few days before my vision quest a friend of mine, Leslie, and I offered prayers, chants, and drumming to all of the directions around a medicine wheel.

I thought my "Cry for Vision" would be hard because I was so weak and my diarrhea so severe. However, the day of my quest, as soon as the sacred pipe ceremony was complete and I entered the sweat lodge to prepare to go out on my vision quest, my diarrhea stopped and never came back.

My "Cry for Vision" was the most beautiful and rewarding vision quest I have experienced so far. The Milky Way was brighter than I had ever seen. As I gazed up at the vast star-map shining above me, the twinkling stars were drawing me into them. The messages I received were clear, precise, and profound.

My brother Tommy appeared to me with a loving message. Some friends of mine who had died from AIDS complications came and asked me to do something special for them. I promised I would carry out their wishes, at the appropriate time.

I was also given tools and symbols to use in healing. I didn't understand the use of the symbols, but was told that in due time I would.

After my vision quest I silently walked back to camp with my eyes down to the ground, not looking at anyone or anything. I was greeted by the men and women who eagerly and lovingly supported me with their prayers, chants, and drumming, while keeping the fire lit and the sweat lodge ready. Without interruption of my space and peace, they walked me to the sweat lodge. Many of the men and women entered the lodge with me as my spirit came back into the earth realm. A total of 58 stone people (sacred rocks) blessed me in the sacred sweat lodge.

After my sweat I silently crawled out of the womb and was guided to the sacred area where I received water, cherries, and bread. These were the most delicious, red, succulent cherries I had ever tasted. As I bit into them, juice dripped down my hands and arms. Once I completed my meal, everyone circled around me and one by one embraced me and welcomed me back.

You don't need to go on a vision quest to seek the truth. Perhaps a period of solitude will help you to reconnect and bring a sense of inner peace to your heart, mind, and spirit, as you embrace the sacredness of all.

I am looking forward to my four–day vision quest. Until then I will cherish my daily ritual of meditation, prayer, being out in nature, and communicating with the various kingdoms.

Karma

When you hear the word karma, what do you think of? Perhaps something bad has happened to you and someone may have said "That is your karma." Or maybe you hurt another person, animal, or Mother Earth and you were told, "You are going to have bad karma." We often hear the word, but what does it really mean?

Karma is an important concept to Buddhism, which teaches that our experiences are the result of our past actions and our present doings. We are responsible for our happiness and misery. We create our own Heaven. We create our own Hell.

Christians view karma as, "As you sow, so you reap." The Hindus see karma as "cause and effect."

Whether you believe in karma or not, would it not be appropriate to be mindful of all you do and say? Would it not be wise to love ALL with an open heart and feel and show gratitude and appreciation?

What Happens When You Die?
Sharon's Near-Death Experience (NDE)

Millions of men, women, and children have had near-death experiences (NDEs). I would like to share mine with you. The following is taken from my book *Sacred Living, Sacred Dying: A Guide to Embracing Life and Death:*

An exercise for you…

Take a slow deep breath in through your nose, then exhale and let out a sigh. Take another deep breath, and as you exhale let go of any fears, tension, or anxiety. Take another deep breath and begin to feel a sense of calm, inner peace, and warmth enter your Being.

Now tap into the rhythm of your heartbeat. Notice the beat or sound of it. For a minute or so, you may even want to tap your hand onto your knee with each beat of your heart. This precious, powerful, sacred beat is your rhythm of life. It is so often taken for granted, or not even noticed. Your rhythm of life, your heartbeat, your spirit, carries you through each day, and it is a miracle because you don't have to do anything. Just be! The rhythm of life makes you and me a miracle. But what happens when it is taken away? If your eyes were closed, gently open them.

The following is my life during 1996, to the first three months of 1997, due to AIDS complications: PCP (Pneumocystic carinii Pneumonia) and MAC/MAI (Mycobacterterium avium Complex):

My life force is weak and dim. I lie helpless in a cold, sterile hospital bed, hooked up to IVs for treatments and transfusions. Implanted in my chest is a Hickman catheter, a special device for TPN feedings and deep within me, a catheter is imbedded, its tubing ending in a bag to collect my urine. As I gasp for air, a nurse hooks me up to oxygen. Each breath of life becomes more precious and difficult.

I have lost my independence. I am no longer capable of caring for myself. I buzz the nurse to adjust my skeletal body, to ease my pain.

A handful of pills, one more shot, one more IV, a familiar face exploring my body. My sheets, gown, pillow, and entire body drenched with sweat. Fevers over 103 degrees. Then chills, as cold as ice. I lie in bed and suddenly start to shake. I close my fists tightly, thinking it is an earthquake. But it isn't an earthquake, it's me, shivering. When will it end? The tubes, the suffering, the emotions and confusion. Is death knocking at my door?

Nothing stays in my body. The stench of vomit and diarrhea envelops me and permeates my surroundings. Why do people call? Why do they come visit me? I'm not the woman they knew. Do they come out of curiosity or to bid their farewells? Too exhausted to return conversation, I fall into a deep sleep. Abruptly, as always, someone wakens me. Their cold hands touch my body as they take my blood pressure and search for a vein to draw blood.

Day in and day out, endlessly the same. Am I living? I fear not. I no longer have a vital quality of life. I would much rather die than live a life in my condition. I am suffering, and so is my family. I know my life is slipping away. Soon I will be united in Spirit with God.

Many times in the past, I wanted my life to end. But I am not ready to die yet. My heart and soul ache for my daughter, Jeaneen. I must embrace her one more time.

I will never forget the night before my near-death experience:

That evening when Jeaneen walked into my hospital room, she stood by the doorway and looked at me as though I were a stranger. As I caught a glimpse of her, the room seemed to light up and a surge of energy came over me. A sense of calm filled my soul as my heart filled with excitement at the sight of Jeaneen. Yet it frightened me that she continued to stand in the doorway. As she stared at me, I realized my thin, pale, pasty body must have been a pathetic sight.

Then within a matter of seconds she burst into tears, dashed towards me, bent over the hospital bed, and put her arms around me. Tears streamed down our cheeks as we embraced one another. I felt my body shake with excitement.

"Mommy! Mommy! I love you!"

I managed to gather what little strength I had to say, "Oh, Honey, I love you."

After regaining what little composure I could muster, she quickly asked, "Mom, can I stay here with you all night?"

My eyes must have gleamed as I said, "Yes!"

She lowered the bed safety rail, sat next to me and held my hand. Softly she placed her hands on my face, looked into my eyes, and told me how much she loved and missed me. Tears of joy rolled down our faces. Jeaneen smiled as she wiped my runny nose with a Kleenex and then lightly rubbed away my teardrops, and hers.

"Oh Mommy, I want to make you well. I want to be able to do things together again. I want to bring you home and take care of you."

I wanted to smile at her, but it felt like a knife had sliced me open and ripped my insides out. Jeaneen asked, "Mom, can I crawl into bed with you and hold you in my arms? I'll try not to move or hurt you." I welcomed her to join me. The warmth of her body next to mine and her hand and arm placed on my chest made me feel safe and loved. "I love you!" I could feel my shoulder get moist from her tears. No words could describe the love we shared for one another. Jeaneen knew the intense love I had for her through my actions, words, support, guidance, and freedom to express herself, which I gave her throughout her life. A loving look, a gentle caress, our special kiss, holding hands as we so often did. These simple things brought me comfort.

Hours passed and we fell asleep in each other's arms. Throughout the night we didn't get much rest. In the morning, when breakfast arrived for Jeaneen, I could tell she was exhausted. After she ate her meal, she asked, "Mom, if you don't mind I would like to drive back to your house and take a shower. I'll be right back. Do you want anything from home?"

I smiled and said, "Just you." I watched as she slowly walked out into the corridor.

My body trembled, and I became weaker. Jeaneen had been lying by my side, but now I was awake and alone—or I thought I was alone! All of a sudden, my Spirit lifted out of me, and it hovered over my physical body in the bed below. I immediately felt healed, more alive and freer than I had ever felt before. Warmth of love and inner peace cascaded from within me.

After my Spirit floated over my body for a short time, two Spirit Beings, one male and one female, appeared before me. They were dressed in long white gowns. They looked to be physical, yet I could see through them, just like my other Spirit Guides who have been with me for so many years.

The Spirit Beings reached out and took my hand. Telepathically, they told me they wanted to show me a review of my life.

In an instant I was taken to different scenes and events in my lifetime with numerous people and situations from around the world. As I was above looking down and witnessing the scenes, telepathically the Spirit Beings said, *"Look at the difference you have made in their lives."* After I had seen numerous events and some people I had forgotten, and the impact I had made on so many lives, the Spirit Beings quickly took me away.

I felt myself upright and horizontally move into, and through a bright Tunnel of Light. I noticed gray figures like people on each side of the tunnel attempting to reach out and touch me. Swiftly I passed unfamiliar faces who looked at me. I wanted to cry out, "Where are my brothers, Tommy and Raymond? Where are my friends and loved ones who have gone before me?" Yet, I was silent.

At what seemed to be the end of the Tunnel there appeared, once again, the most immense, beautiful, warm, brilliant, radiant, loving light shining upon me and enveloping me. It was the same Light I saw when I attempted to commit suicide. I was awed by the beauty, peace, and serenity. Telepathically, from the Light of God, I heard, *"My Child, unlike the time before, you have a choice. You can come with me or you can return and continue your life."* The silent, loving, telepathic voice of Infinite Spirit went on to say,

"Before you make your decision, I want to show you one more thing."

Instantaneously, I relived—not reviewed, but *relived*—my life with Jeaneen. I felt her in my womb; I felt the sensation of her first kick within me; I rubbed my tummy, sang to her and told her how much I loved her before she was even born. Then, I relived her actual birth, felt her tiny lips suck on my breasts. I listened to her gurgles and coos. I smelled the wonderful scent of my baby from her first bath. I relived numerous experiences and special times with Jeaneen, throughout her 21 years. There was laughter, playfulness, tears, as well as the challenges we had shared together through our life journey. There were moments when we were not only mother and daughter, but friends, companions, spiritual teachers, and so much more to one another. We felt blessed to be together.

A spark of Light hit me, and once again I appeared before the Light of God. Telepathically, I was asked, *"My Child, what is your decision?"*

The intense love, healing, and peace I felt in the Light of Infinite Spirit was so profound. Yet silently, I thought, I cannot leave Jeaneen. Not yet! I expressed in sincere love, "I have to return to my daughter."

Immediately and without warning, I was in the hospital bed. My deteriorated body still looked like a corpse. However, I was alive! Tears of joy streamed down my cheeks. For the next hour, my entire Being glowed with love and light. As I closed my eyes, I could see bursts of Light go into every cell, sparkling and vibrating with energy. The healing power of God was restoring me cell by cell. The sensation felt like effervescent bubbles. It was as if I were being newly created with life, strength, and energy. The intense surge and vibrant life force running through me was so strong I knew before long I would be back home, in my Earthly home, healthy!

I had reclaimed my life, and my entire Being glowed with love for Jeaneen and life. Silently I prayed, "Thank you, Infinite Spirit for my life and for Jeaneen. Thank you for this moment of life, however brief or long it may be."

Before me appeared new beginnings, dreams, fresh goals, freedom, health, serenity, inner peace, and love.

A few days later in meditation, I asked why I didn't see Tommy and Raymond, and I was told, *"My Child, if you saw the one you call Tommy your decision might have been harder."*

The next day Tommy appeared to me as he had in the past. He said, *"Sharon, you do not have to die to be with me. I am always with you and I love you."*

Jeaneen's love brought me back to life. She is my hero! In a matter of weeks I was home and in the loving care and hands of Jeaneen and my sister Joyce. However, within six months I moved to San Diego, California to once again be a member of the AIDS Community.

Before departing to San Diego, I asked in meditation, "What is my life purpose now? Do I continue to teach people around the world about HIV/AIDS, mind-body-spirit, and eating disorders?"

What I clearly heard was, *"Yes My Child, but there is more. Do what you know the best. Go back to the beginning where you comforted and assisted men who were dying. Because of you their stories live on. It is time to break the silence about dying and death and bring back the sacredness of life and death. Write a book and share your wisdom. Once again you will travel the world."*

❖ In 2006, I was guided to write and publish my first book, *Sacred Living, Sacred Dying: A Guide to Embracing Life and Death.* It is a step-by-step book filled with valuable and heartfelt questions about your life journey. The questions assist you to tap into your precious memories hidden in the back roads of your mind and bring them forward to create a legacy for your friends and loved ones.

After recording your legacy, the questions and suggestions in the book guide you to create a unique memorial, celebration, or funeral which will represent your life story and personality. This allows your friends and loved ones to celebrate your life, rather than mourn your death. It also spares others from having to make critical and often difficult decisions at an emotional time.

When people create their legacy and memorial they stop taking life for granted. They start to reprioritize their life.

They discover and experience an inner peace about dying and death. They embrace the sacredness of life and death, and they allow their precious memories to live on for future generations.

* * *

Now take a slow deep breath in and release it. Your breath has not become silent. Listen to it. Notice your breath of life. Notice the rhythm, the beat and the sound of your precious heart. This is your rhythm of life. Do not take life for granted. Honor your life force and give homage to it. Life is Sacred and so is Death.

You do not have to be at the threshold of death to receive the lessons.

ॐ   ॐ

Heaven

What is heaven? Is it a place high in the sky? Is it paradise, eternal life, or the kingdom of God?

The Bible and Christians believe all of the above. What if heaven is a state of mind? Many times throughout my life I have experienced a feeling of heaven. These are times when I am attuned and absorbed within the perfection of the Oneness of all, and the presence of Infinite Spirit all around me. A deep sense of inner peace, joy, tranquility, and love radiates around and through me. Can this not be heaven on Earth—a place within you?

While on this Earth plane why not open your heart with no resistance or judgment, which allows your light to shine brighter? Look inward. Feel your heart radiate with love—let the gates of heaven open up. Let love shine.

If God is within us, and there is no separation, is not heaven within us also? When you quiet yourself, the voice comes from within, not from above.

Perhaps there are various ways to look at heaven.

Past Lives

Past lives, do they exist? A lot of religions don't believe in past lives. However, there are a lot of cultures and religions that do believe in them. Whatever you believe, I would like to share my experience.

Growing up I was fearful of cats. It didn't matter if it was a kitten or older cat. I hated them and feared them. A friend of mine studied hypnosis, and I asked her to work with me on why I was so fearful of cats.

She took me into meditation and then hypnotized me. This is what I saw and experienced:

❖ I went back to my childhood, into the womb, and then back to the Roman Empire. I saw everything as real as I see things that are before me now—the sounds, smells, images, the clothing, and colors. I was a townsman deeply in love with a beautiful woman who belonged to an emperor. (The woman turned out to be my former husband, Sid, in this lifetime.) The emperor had a lot of woman by his side. This woman and I had to sneak around to be together. Once the Emperor found out about us he made me (the man) an offer. "You can take her as your wife but only if you fight the lions." I knew it would be a challenge, but I was up for it. She was the love of my life, and I wanted to make her my wife and live together forever.

The entire arena was filled with spectators. As I entered the grounds I looked up at her and my heart was filled with love. Suddenly the gate opened and a lion came toward me. Then another and another. There were three mighty hungry lions eating the flesh of my body. I died in the name of love.

A few months after my past life regression, a beautiful brown, yellow, black, and white cat with bright green eyes came to Jeaneen's and my home. Jeaneen asked if we could keep her. I said no, but we would feed her until we found the owner. I wasn't afraid of this cat. We never found an owner, so we kept the cat and named her Jade. To our surprise, it wasn't long after Jade moved in that she gave birth to two beautiful kittens in Jeaneen's closet. One was black and white which we called Polarity, the other one was gold and white, which we called Golden Ray.

I truly believe if it hadn't been for my past life regression, Jade never would have come to me. I also believe that Jade, Polarity, and Golden Ray and I met back in the Roman Empire days in the center of the arena. This was truly a healing, and I now enjoy playing and being around cats. I also reunited with the woman in my Roman lifetime as my former husband, Sid, in this lifetime. Sid and I also had a Native American life together.

❖ I have also had other past life regressions that helped me understand and release emotions concerning my grandfather. There were many lifetimes my grandfather and I came together playing different roles and sexes.

❖ In several life times with my grandfather, Jeaneen was also present. One time I was married to my grandfather and he was a drunk and repeatedly beat me. Jeaneen (as a woman) worked in the market place and we became close friends. However, we couldn't spend much time together because of the control my husband had over me. When I didn't make my regular trips to the market, somehow Jeaneen (the woman) knew my husband (grandfather) had beat me, and she would leave flowers on my door step.

❖ Because my brother Tommy's and my connection to one another was so strong, years after he died I took the time to have a past life regression regarding our connection. Through hypnosis I was brought back to Colonial times where I lived in a large mansion, wore beautiful long gowns, and Tommy was in a military uniform. He wasn't my brother, but my lover. The love between us was tremendous!

There were various scenes I relived with Tommy, but the last one I saw was down by a lake. We were standing under a weeping willow tree. The sun was shining and he held me in his arms. As we faced one another we could feel the intense love between us. We looked into each others eyes with love and joy, and yet I felt and saw sorrow. Tears rolled down my cheek. There was no separation between us. It was a love I had never felt before.

Then all of a sudden I heard a voice say, *"You cannot see anymore,"* and I was immediately pulled out of the scene. I remember I cried for hours longing to be with this man—my brother in this lifetime. I was told if I would not have left the scene at that moment, I would have had a difficult time coming back into this lifetime.

I know people who live in their past lives. Past life regression can be beneficial if you have an unresolved issue, and you believe the cause may be due to a past life. However, do not stop living this life because of who you were in a past life.

Past life regressions have also proven helpful for people with unexplained pain, emotions, and various phobias.

If you would like to read about reincarnation, there is an amazing book I would recommend by Brian Weiss, *Many Lives, Many Masters.*

Whether you believe in past lives or not, have you ever met someone or been somewhere that was so familiar to you that you had to question when, where, and how?

The moment I walked into the store where Hector worked, I felt an energy shift within myself. It was so intense and pure. Later on as we dated, he mentioned and still does that he knew we have always been together and always will.

I know if I did a past life regression concerning Hector and me, it would be magical, loving, spiritual, breathtaking, and powerful!

☙ ❧

An Opening Ceremony

When I work with groups of people, I like to open with various ceremonies. I found it is extremely important to connect with one another from the heart center because it brings balance, harmony, and purpose for the group as a whole. The following is one expression which unites everyone. I received this ceremony in the late 1980s, and I'm sorry I don't know who to acknowledge for the creation.

❖ This opening ceremony can be done while everyone is in a circle or across from one another.

1. I offer you peace. (Face palms forward, elbows bent.)

2. I offer you friendship. (Cup hands palm to palm, elbows bent.)

3. I offer you love. (Draw hands forward from heart.)

4. I hear your needs. (Cup hands behind ears.)

5. I see your beauty. (Cover eyes with hands, then uncover.)

6. I feel your feelings. (Arms cross chest, fingertips to shoulders. Right hand on top.)

7. My wisdom flows from a Higher Source. (Move right hand up to the crown chakra, palm up, from head past face to meet facing left palm at chest.)

8. I salute the Divinity in you. (Palms together in prayer position.)

9. Let us work together. (Fingers interlocked as two-handed fist.)

Burning Bowl Ceremony

The Burning Bowl Ceremony is a symbolic way to cleanse your life—to rid yourself of the old and replace it with a new way to view yourself and your world.

I have taken all of my challenges, faced them, and released them (burned them), which has allowed me to heal and become the woman I am today. In other words, my ashes (past challenges) have become sacred. I have been blessed by these challenges because they have healed me and brought me to self-discovery, wholeness, and living my life purpose.

Throughout my years of healing, I have used the "Burning Bowl Ceremony" to release negative things. I would like to share this ceremony with you, in hopes that you, too, may discover through your ashes, something sacred.

* * *

You can use the Burning Bowl Ceremony to release negativity such as fears, limiting thoughts, anger, self-doubt, or resentment. Or you can use the ceremony to bring about positive things in your life. If you decide to use the Burning Bowl Ceremony for something positive, be sure you are specific on what it is you want. Also, ask that it be for your highest good, or if it includes others, that it be for the highest good of all concerned.

I will give you a couple of examples of what I have seen happen when you are not specific. I attended a retreat, and my positive focus was on writing a book. I visualized using all my senses on being a writer and all that went along with it. When I returned from the retreat, the first call I received was from a man who wanted to know if I could write his life story. Silently, I laughed. I knew I was not specific in my desire. Yes, I wanted to write, but I wanted to write and publish my stories. Immediately, I changed my desires and was extremely specific on what I wanted.

Remember your words are your power. Another example was a friend of mine who kept putting out that she wanted a new car. Before long she received a new car, but it came about due to a horrible car accident in which she was involved. She learned when she received her car it would have been for her highest good to be open to receive the car or money as a gift from the Universe without pain or suffering.

I hope you can see from these two examples how important it is to frame your words and desires in a positive way, being specific.

* * *

To Prepare for the Burning Bowl Ceremony you will need the following items: A pen or pencil, lightweight paper such as onion skin which releases less smoke, and a metal pan or bowl with a sturdy stand or base. You may want to put dirt or sand in the bottom of the pan or bowl. If you don't have the proper bowl you can use your sink, a fire pit, or anything in which it would be safe to burn paper. You will also need a screen to cover the top to prevent ashes from escaping, as well as matches, lighter, candle, or some other means of lighting the paper, and a fire extinguisher for safety. Don't put the container on carpet or other inflammable material.

The Ritual: The Burning Bowl Ceremony is a symbolic way to cleanse your life. The fire in the Burning Bowl is a symbol of transformation. The fire takes the paper and changes it from one form to another. As you write down things like your blocks, fears, mistakes, and old hurts, and then burn them, you change and release the form that once held you. By doing so it allows you to experience your personal power, freeing you to work and live your life in a positive, conscious, and empowering way.

Before you begin your process, create a special space for your ceremony. You may choose to light a candle, play soft music, say a prayer of intent to release, or be receptive for that which is truly for your highest good or for all concerned.

Sit in a comfortable position. Gently close your eyes and take a couple of deep breaths. Begin to allow yourself to bring into your consciousness the things you want to release, or the things you desire. Open your eyes and write the things that came to your mind. Then close your eyes again and take another deep breath. Notice if there is anything you want to add. If so, write it down.

When you have finished writing, ignite your paper and put it in the container. Sit in silence and watch the flames as they turn what you have released (or asked for) into ashes. This is the symbol of transformation. You let go of the old and allow yourself to bring in the new.

As the different colors of the flame dance and engulf your words, notice your body sensations.

After your words have been transformed into *"sacred ashes,"* visualize, imagine, or sense how your life will be different. Incorporate as many senses as you can into your visualization.

Once the fire has gone out you can discard your ashes any way you wish, such as bury them, flush them down the toilet, or crush them and then blow them into the air. Know you have released them to Infinite Spirit and the Universe. Give thanks for the healing and blessing that occurred.

Allow the Burning Bowl Ceremony, the flame, and ashes to be a transformation. My blessings to you, as you turn your challenges into s*acred ashes.*

꙳   ꙳

Namasté

I want to close my book with my favorite word—Namasté.

Namasté is pronounced "Na-ma-stay," and is a combination of two Sanskrit words, namas, and te. The word "Namas" means "bow, or salutation." "Te" means "to you." All together, "Namasté" means "I bow to you."

The word Namasté can elevate one's consciousness, reminding a person that existence is sacred. Namasté is normally used in Nepal and India by Buddhists, Hindus, Sikhs, and Jains. However, more people in the Western World are using it as sincere greeting.

The gesture of Namasté represents the belief that there is a Divine spark within each of us that is located in the heart chakra. The gestures I learned for Namasté are to place my hands together at my heart chakra, close my eyes, and bow my head. It can also be done by placing your hands together in front of your third eye, bowing your head, and then bringing your hands down to the heart. This is a deep form of respect. If this gesture is done with deep feeling in your heart and with your mind surrendered, a deep union of Spirits can be felt and experienced.

Namasté can be used in the following ways:

❖ I honor and worship the Divine in all.

❖ I salute the divinity within you.

❖ I honor in you the Divine that I honor within myself, and I know we are one.

❖ I honor the light in you that is the same in me.

When I attended the Artist's Way Workshop, at the closing, we acknowledged one another by bowing and saying:

> Namasté.
> I honor the place in you in which the entire Universe dwells.
> I honor the place in you which is of love, of truth, of light, and of peace.
> When you are in that place in you, I am in that place in me.
> We are One.

Simple, yet a powerful word to be shared with all.

Namasté.

Closing Thoughts

From the center of my heart, I want to thank you for allowing me to share the mind-body-spirit healing techniques that have enhanced my life and well-being. May you embrace the modalities that resonate with you and experience your True Essence. Live your life with passion. You are a Magnificent Being!

Remember, <u>you</u> hold the answers within you and these tools can help you access your higher wisdom. Look within! Let your Spirit soar, as you embrace your truth!

If you would like to contact me for speaking engagements, book signings, workshops, presentations, or for any other reason, please visit my website at www.sharonlund.com. I would love to hear from you!

A CD of the affirmations, visualizations, and processes are available for sale on my website.

May your journey through life be filled with inner peace, happiness, health, and love as you listen to the inner and higher wisdom of your Mind-Body-Spirit.

Namasté,

Sharon

Sharon

I Open My Heart of Gratefulness

As I journeyed with the creation of *The Integrated Being: Techniques to Heal Your Mind-Body-Spirit,* there were several people who made it possible to move forward with my book with ease and grace. With love and affection, I open my heart of gratefulness:

❖ The creator of ALL—God—and to all my teachers and the essence of life itself.

❖ My heart is wide open as I express my deep love and gratitude to my mom and dad, Jean and Tom, without whom my life would not have come into this existence. I chose the perfect parents for my life experiences.

❖ Jeaneen, you are the light of my life and the reason I am alive. I cherish the loving connection we have as mother, daughter, student, teacher, and friends. You are my inspiration and sacred gift from Infinite Spirit. Thank you for choosing me to birth you.

❖ Joyce, Infinite Spirit blessed me with a wonderful, loving sister and I want to thank you for always being there for me. I am proud to be called your sister. I love you!

❖ Hector, you held a crystal clear vision and sacred space for me to birth *The Integrated Being.* Thank you for your eternal love and support. From the center of my heart, I deeply and completely love you.

292

❧ ❧

My Wonderful Supporters

❖ Stuart Altschuler, Dr. Nathaniel Branden, Christine Dreher, Linda Dutton-Steindler, Sally Fisher, Susan Gregg, Rev. Roxie Hart, Christine McMaster, and Valerie Seeman Moreton, thank you for giving me permission to use portions of your material, so I could share your wisdom and teachings with the readers. I acknowledge you for the wonderful work and services you provide to humanity, and all I have learned from you.

❖ Bhaswati Bhattacharya, M.D., Gerald Jampolsky, M.D., Stephen and Ondrea Levine, and Christiane Northrup, M.D., you are extensions of goodwill bearing witness to the oneness—many facets of the wholeness—all messengers from the same source expressed through each of us. You nourish, inspire, and bring words to create peace, love, joy, contentment, and healing in the human community, while also integrating with our authentic nature and extending and merging to all that is. You have made a profound difference with your wisdom and gifts to humanity. Thank you for appreciating and honoring me with your kind words for my latest book.

❖ Bhaswati, you have a unique, beautiful, and uplifting way of relating to people and bringing forth spiritual and healing wisdom. I know the knowledge in your upcoming book will touch millions of lives. I am honored to call you my friend!

❖ Jerry, throughout the world men, women, and children have been blessed by applying your positive teachings during times of crisis—including me!

❖ Stephen and Ondrea, for decades you have made a profound difference in my life. Your workshops, books, and inspiration assisted me through some of my most difficult times. Thank you both for sharing your truth. In my heart I will cherish your friendship forever, as your legacy lives on!

❖ Christiane, I am blessed to know you and see you as a leader, mentor, and inspirational speaker on health, wellness, and women's issues. Thank you for the gift of *Women's Bodies, Women's Wisdom!*

My Amazing Book Team

❖ Candace Boeck, thank you for editing the first draft of my manuscript. You taught me a lot about words and editing.

❖ David Bolduc, thank you for your research assistance. You taught me valuable information.

❖ Andrea Glass, thank you for your expertise in the industry, and your eagle eye, as your suggestions enhanced my book.

❖ Robert Goodman and Lynette Smith, thank you for assisting me with formatting my manuscript. Lynette, thank you for taking time to teach me how to work with some of the hidden tools. What I learned from you will make my next book easier to format.

❖ Monica Hagen, my editor, you are a bright light who has lasered through my words and made sure they sparkled. Thank you for your loving support, friendship, and for helping me birth *The Integrated Being*. Your insights and compassion made the process easier. I look forward to working with you on my next project—*Dying to Live: NDE* documentary.

❖ Kari Ann Luevano, thank you for doing a beautiful job with my hair and make up. You made me feel comfortable as you brought forth my beauty.

❖ Jeaneen Lund, you are an extremely gifted, talented, and versatile photographer with a keen eye for uniqueness and creativity. Thank you for capturing the "true essence" of your mom—ME!

❖ Wendee Mason, thank you for your skills in marketing and for evaluating my first cover and making suggestions for a new one. You provided me with some wonderful ideas and inspired me to recreate my cover so it would bring out the essence of who I am and my healing message.

❖ Miko Radcliff, I feel blessed for our continued friendship and for your expertise in creating not only the cover for *The Integrated Being*, but also *Sacred Living, Sacred Dying: A Guide to Embracing Life and Death*. Once again you embraced my vision and brought it into reality. I love what you created. Thank you for sharing your talent as a graphic design artist.

❖ The entire staff at Lightning Source, I want to thank you for your support and guidance in printing my book.

☙   ❧

My Loving and Inspirational Friends

❖ Life would not be the same without my global circle of friends. My heart is filled with gratitude to the following men and women who have supported me during the development and birthing of *The Integrated Being: Techniques to Heal Your Mind-Body-Spirit:* Sandra Beck, Andre Carter, Tianna Conte, Lois Dietrich, Gail Dickson, Neil Evanson, jacki gethner, Rev. Roxie Hart, Judy Jewel, Carol Klink, Susan Lawson, Vicki Leon, Steven Lowe, Dorothy Mahrie, HHP, Melissa Noble, D.O., Carol Powell, Bonnie Sabb, Diane Shea, Marlena Shell, Clinton Swaine, Sharon Thompson, Wanda Wainman, and Susan Wellborn, FNP. I feel honored to know you!

❖ Controversial Bookstore, Owners Claudia and Doug Kimball, my friends Leslie Martin, Tamara McCullough, Arlen Keane, Erica Jemison-Baltzar, Barbara Klein DD., and the rest of the staff, thank you for allowing me to bounce off ideas, thoughts, designs, and photos for *The Integrated Being* with you. I deeply appreciate your friendship, support, knowledge, and encouragement.

APPENDIX

OTHER VALUABLE RESOURCES

When I read my final manuscript before sending it to be published, I realized it would not be complete without including the following:

BOOKS

Along with every book I mentioned in the main text of *The Integrated Being: Techniques to Heal Your Mind-Body-Spirit,* the following books have also been particularly helpful. This list is not complete by any means:

- ❖ Anodea, Judith, PhD. *Eastern Body, Western Mind.* Explore the psychology of the chakras.

- ❖ Bradshaw, John. *Healing the Shame That Binds You.* A timeless book that assists in healing the past—whether from addictions, abuse, and so much more.

- ❖ Burroughs, Tony. *The Code: Ten Intensions for a Better World.* The title says it all.

- ❖ Campbell, Susan. *10 Truth Skills You Need to Live an Authentic Life.* Easy skills to be authentic.

- ❖ Chopra, Deepak MD. *Creating Health: How To Wake Up the Body's Intelligence.* Deepak creates a new understanding of health, illness, and the power of the mind to heal.

❖ Chopra, Deepak MD. *Quantum Healing: Exploring the Frontiers of Mind/Body Medicine.* This book was first published in the early 1990s. This was one of the first books I read in the field of Psychoneuroimmunology. It combines metaphysics, physics, and medicine to uncover the amazing power of the mind to heal.

❖ Cohen, Alan. *The Dragon Doesn't Live Here Anymore: Living Fully, Loving Freely.* This is one of the first books I read by Alan, and I have enjoyed all of his other books.

❖ Dossey, Larry Dr. *Healing Words: The Power of Prayer and the Practice of Medicine.* A breakthrough in combining the spiritual with the medical. Spirituality and medicine are no longer separate and the book shows the power of affirmative prayer.

❖ Dossey, Larry Dr. *The Extraordinary Healing Power of Ordinary Things: Fourteen Natural Steps to Health and Happiness.* "Dossey encourages us to align ourselves with the wisdom of nature and allow true healing to take place."

❖ Dossey, Larry Dr. *The Power of Premonitions: How Knowing the Future Shapes Our Lives.*

❖ Dyer, Wayne W. *Change Your Thoughts Change Your Life: Living the Wisdom of the Tao.* The book presents 81 essays on how to apply ancient wisdom into your life with practical action steps.

❖ Gawain, Shakti. *Living in the Light: A Guide to Personal and Planetary Transformation.* Learn to listen to your intuition and follow it. Embrace your disowned energies. I recommend all of Shakti Gawian's books.

❖ Gilbert, Elizabeth. *Eat, Pray Love: One Woman's Search for Everything Across Italy, India and Indonesia.* Be kind and nurture yourself.

❖ Goldman, Jonathan. *The 7 Secrets of Sound Healing.* Details, components, and aspects of healing, including exercises and a CD on Vibrational Science.

❖ Grabhorn, Lynn. *Excuse Me, Your Life Is Waiting: The Astonishing Power of Feelings.* Importance of your feelings and deliberate creation.

❖ Jampolsky, Gerald MD. *Love is Letting Go of Fear.* A timeless book in the transpersonal movement. Includes 12 daily progressive lessons for transformation.

❖ Katie, Byron. *Loving What Is: Four Questions That Can Change Your Life.* I have used her four questions and they have transformed my belief to what is reality.

❖ Kuhn Truman, Karol. *Feelings Buried Alive Never Die.* Tracks the origin of your emotions, with simple tools to release negative feelings.

❖ MacLeod, Ainslie. *The Instruction: Living the Life Your Soul Intended.* A step-by-step program for realizing your personal fulfillment.

❖ McGarey, William A. MD. *The Edgar Cayce Remedies.* Treats the total person—mentally, physically, and spiritually.

❖ Millman, Dan. *The Life You Were Born to Live: A Guide to Finding Your Life Purpose.* When I used Dan's book I discovered I am doing exactly what I am meant to do. An amazing book with a lot of insights.

❖ Myss, Carolyn PhD. *Why People Don't Heal and How They Can.* Uncovering the blocks to heal our life.

❖ Peck, Scott M. *The Road Less Traveled: A New Psychology of Love, Traditional Values and Spiritual Growth.* This is one of the first spiritual books I read in the early 1980s. Since 2003 Scott has had his 25th anniversary edition available.

❖ Pert, Candace B. *Molecules of Emotions: The Science Behind Mind-Body Medicine.* A true story of Candace's life as a conventional scientist who embraced alternative and complementary medicine. Strong scientific support in mind-body cellular communication.

❖ Ponder, Catherine. *Open Your Mind to Receive.* An easy to understand book on how to open up to receive and the necessary steps to take.

❖ Romeyn, Mary MD. *Nutrition and HIV: A New Model for Treatment.* Published in 1998, this book focuses on the needs of those living with HIV/AIDS.

❖ Shinn Scovel, Florence. *The Wisdom of Florence Scovel Shinn.* This is a set of timeless books with an easy-to-grasp explanation of success principles. Included are

Florence's following books: *The Game of Life and How to Play It, The Power of the Spoken Word, Your Word is Your Wand,* and *The Secret of Success.*

❖ Siegel, Bernie S MD. *Love, Medicine & Miracles.* Mind-body relationships in healing. Also shares some of his cancer patient's health journey.

❖ Sutherland, Caroline M. *The Body Knows: How to Tune In to Your Body and Improve Your Health.* "Understanding the terrain of the physical, emotional, and spiritual components of vibrant health."

❖ Tolle, Eckhart. *A New Earth: Awakening to Your Life's Purpose* (Oprah's Book Club.) How essential it is to transcend our ego based state of consciousness and awaken to a new state of consciousness.

❖ Tolle, Eckhart. *The Power of Now: A Guide To Spiritual Enlightenment.* How to use your creative mind, live in the moment, and use the power. An easy-to-understand book with questions and answers.

❖ Vertosick, Frank. T. Jr. *The Genius Within: Discovering the Intelligence of Every Living Thing.* Simple to understand and effective exercises to reach the sub-conscious mind.

❖ Weil, Andrew MD. *Natural Health, Natural Medicine: The Complete Guide to Wellness and Self-Care for Optimum Health.* Filled with valuable home remedies, practical tips, resources, and so much more.

❖ Williamson, Marianne. *Illuminata: A Return to Prayer.* When I find myself in a difficult situation, sometimes I will read a prayer from Marianne's book.

❖ Woodland, Lynn. *Power Effectiveness and Spirit a New Paradigm: Human Potential and Practical Steps to Achieving it.* Leap of consciousness.

❖ Yogananda, Paramahansa. *Autobiography of a Yogi.* His life story.

ॐ ॐ

AFFIRMATION AND ORACLE CARDS

In our everyday lives we get so caught up in activities that inspirational and insightful cards can bring us back into balance, and help us experience peace. You can use these cards for affirmations, meditations, answers to your questions, or just the pleasure of an uplifting message and beautiful image.

- ❖ Sylvia Browne—renowned psychic has *Heart and Soul Cards* "with a variety of topics (grief, joy, strength, nutrition, etc.) that will warm your heart and soul and give you insight into the true meaning of life."

- ❖ Deepak Chopra—has 50 *Success Cards,* "to inspire you to further tap in to the metaphysical wonder of creating success and money."

- ❖ Dr. Wayne W. Dyer—*10 Secrets for Success and Inner Peace Cards,* "are based on his best-selling book. The 50 principles on the tranquil cards can guide you to a sense of inner peace and empowerment."

- ❖ Stephen D. Farmer, Ph.D.—has a set of 44 cards and guidebook *Power Animals,* "which are spirit guides in animal form who will advise you about any aspect of your life."

- ❖ Louise L. Hay's—50 *Healthy Body Cards* "is filled with affirmations designed to make you feel good about every part of your body."

❖ Esther and Jerry Hicks—present the teaching of the non-physical entities known as Abraham, in their 60 *Ask and It Is Given Cards.* "Capture the essence of the life-changing best-selling book *Ask and It Is Given.* A gentle stroll through these cards will return you to your personal power."

❖ Denise Linn—*Soul Coaching Oracle Cards: What Your Soul Wants to Know.* With Denise's 52 cards and guidebook, "You'll come to understand what your soul wants you to know about your relationships, your career, your creativity and even future."

❖ Caroline Myss and Peter Occhiogrosso—*Healing Cards: A Daily Practice for Maintaining Spiritual Balance* is a set of 50 cards and a booklet. "Each card presents healing wisdom drawn from the world's great spiritual traditions, and offer an application of knowledge for everyday living."

❖ Christiane Northrup, MD—has a set of 50 illustrated cards and booklet, *Women's Bodies, Women's Wisdom: Healing Cards,* "to help women reach clarity, fulfillment, and success in each five major life areas: Fertility and Creativity, Partnership, Self-Expression, Self-Care and Nutrition, and development of an Enlightened Mind and Heart."

❖ Gary R. Renard—has created *Enlightenment Cards: Thoughts from The Disappearance of the Universe,* "spoken from his Ascended Master Teachers. The 72-card deck is to accelerate your spiritual growth."

❖ Cheryl Richardson—has exquisite art work on each of her 50 *Grace Cards*, "to assist you to work with the Divine energy."

❖ Don Miguel Ruiz, with Jane Mills—shares the Toltec Wisdom in *The Four Agreements*. "He reminds us of a profound and simple truth: The only way to end our emotional suffering and restore our joy in living is to stop believing in lies—mainly about ourselves. In his 48 cards, he shows us how to recover our faith in the truth and return to our own common sense."

❖ Jamie Sams and David Carson's—*Medicine Cards: The Discovery of Power Through the Ways of Animals*, "has 54 beautifully illustrated Medicine Shield cards, including 44 power animals cards and 9 cards for personal use, plus 224-page illustrated hardcover book. Discover your power through the ways of animals! Learn to see your path on Mother Earth more clearly using a divination system which is grounded in ancient wisdom."

❖ In 2008, I was introduced to the *Virtues Project* and I really like what they offer to humanity. The *Virtues Project* was founded in 1991 by Linda Kavelin Popov, Dr. Dan Popov, and John Kavelin. It is a global grassroots initiative to inspire the practice of virtues in all aspects of life. The Project is a catalyst for the renewal of kindness, justice, and integrity in more than 90 countries and was honored by the United Nations during the International Year of the Family as a "model global program for families of all cultures."

The *Virtues Project* inspires individuals to live more authentic, joyful lives, families to raise children of compassion and integrity, educators to create safe, caring, and high performing learning communities, and leaders to inspire excellence and ethics in the workplace.

The Five Strategies are the signature contribution of the *Virtues Project*. They are based on the virtues that are universally valued by all cultures and faiths.

Virtues cards are a great tool to use to strengthen our virtues and connect more deeply with others. *Virtues Reflection Cards* come in a set of 100 full color cards which feature photographs of natural beauty from around the globe. They are written for adults to use in daily reflection. A Virtues Pick either in a sharing circle or in our quiet time helps us to focus on cultivating the virtues more deeply.

The *Virtues Project* Educator's Cards are inspirational reminders and affirmations that are a simple, yet powerful tool to use in your family, classroom, counseling session, sharing circle, corporate team, or in your own reflection corner.

To learn more about The Virtues Project visit http://www.virtuesproject.com. To purchase virtue cards or other virtues project materials visit www.heartofeducation.net/Products.html.

ﾥ ﾥ

SUPPORT AND RESOURCES

ABUSE

ﾥ ﾥ

Childhelp USA® National Child Abuse Hotline
1-800-4-A-CHILD® (1-800-422-4453)
Hours: 24 hours a day, 7 days a week
Serving the United States, Canada, U.S. Virgin Islands,
Puerto Rico, and Guam.
Offers three-way calling and
communication in 140 languages.
http://www.childhelpusa.org

ﾥ ﾥ

Elder or Dependent Adult Abuse Hotline
888-436-3600

ﾥ ﾥ

National Center for Victims of Crime Helpline
1-800-394-2255 or TTY: 1-800-211-7996
Serving victims in more than 150 languages.
Hours: Monday through Friday, 8:30 am – 8:30 pm
(Eastern Time)
http://www.ncvc.org

ࠇ ࠆ

National Coalition Against Domestic Violence Hotline
800-799-7233 or TTY 800-787-3224
Hours: 24 hours a day, 7 days a week
Se Hablo Espanol
http://www.ncadv.org

ࠇ ࠆ

National Domestic Violence Hotline
1-800-799-7233 or TTY: 1-800-787-3224
Hours: 24 hours a day, 7 days a week
http://www.ndvh.org

ࠇ ࠆ

Prevent Child Abuse America
312-663-3520
Hours: 9:00 am – 5:00 pm, Monday-Friday (Central Time)
http://www.preventchildabuse.org

ࠇ ࠆ

Rape Abuse and Incest National Network (RAINN)
1-800-656-Hope or 1-800-656- 4673
TTY: 1-800-810-7440
Hours: 24 hours a day, 7 days a week
http:/www.rainn.org

ADDICTIONS

ॐ ॐ

AL ANON (and **ALATEEN** for younger members):
1-800-4AL-ANON (1-888-425-2666), in Canada and the USA
Hours: Monday through Friday 8:00 am to 6:00 pm
(Eastern Time)
A worldwide organization offering a self-help recovery program
for families and friends of alcoholics
whether or not the alcoholic seeks help
or even recognizes the existence of a drinking problem.

ॐ ॐ

Alcoholics Anonymous (AA)
General Service Office
475 Riverside Drive, 11th Floor
New York, NY 10115
212-870-3400
Hours: 8:30 am - 4:45 pm, Monday-Friday (Eastern Time)
Alcoholics Anonymous groups can be found
in the white pages of your local phone book.
http://www.alcoholics-annoymous.org

ॐ ॐ

Children of Alcoholics Foundation
http://www.coaf.org

ॐ ॐ

Cocaine Anonymous
National referral line: 1-800-347-8998

ক্ষ ক্ষ

Co-Dependents Anonymous World Services, Inc.
http://www.wscoda.org

ক্ষ ক্ষ

Gam-Anon International Service Office
718-352-1671
Twelve-step, self-help program for family, friends, and loved
ones of someone who has a gambling problem.
http://www.gam-anon.org

ক্ষ ক্ষ

Gamblers Anonymous International Directory
Select an area of the world to find a Gamblers Anonymous
meeting near you.
Open and closed meetings.
http://www.gamblersanonymous.org/mtgdirTOP.html

ক্ষ ক্ষ

National Council on Alcoholism and Drug Dependence Helpline
1-800-622-2255
Counseling and treatment.
Put in your zip code location near you.
http://www.ncadd.org

ক্ষ ক্ষ

The Society for the Advancement of Sexual Health (SASH)
770-541-9912

Hope and valuable resources for those seeking information about sexual addictions.
http://www.sash.net

৯ৎ ৵৯

National Institute of Drug Abuse (NIDA)
301-443-6245
800-662-4357 Treatment Referral Routing Center
Hours: Monday through Friday 8:30 am – 5:00 pm
(Eastern Time)
http://www.drugabuse.gov

৯ৎ ৵৯

Nar-Anon Family Group Headquarters, Inc.
22527 Crenshaw Blvd #200B
Torrance, CA 90505 USA

310-534-8188 or 800-477-6291

FAX 310-534-8688

Twelve-step, self-help program for family, friends and loved ones of someone who has a narcotic problem.

৯ৎ ৵৯

Narcotics Anonymous
1-818-773-9999
Hours: Monday through Friday 8:00 am to 5:00 pm
(Pacific Time)
http://www.na.org

કૐ ৺

Overeaters Anonymous
505-891-2664
http://www.oa.org

ক৐ ৺

Sex Addicts Anonymous
1-800-477-8191
Hours: Monday through Friday 11:00 am to 7:00 pm
(Eastern Time)

ক৐ ৺

Sexual Compulsives Anonymous
1-800-977-HEAL (1-800-977-4325)

ASSOCIATIONS, SOCIETIES, ORGANIZATIONS

ক৐ ৺

American Cancer Society
1-800-227-2345
Hours: 24 hours a day, 7 days a week

ক৐ ৺

American Diabetes Association
1-800-342-2383
Hours: Monday through Friday 8:30 am – 8:00 pm
(Eastern Time)

৯০ ৬

The Americans With Disabilities Act Information and Assistance Hotline (ADA)
1-800-514-0301
TTY: 1-800-514-0383
International: 1-202-541-0301
Hours: Monday through Thursday 12:30 pm to 5:30 pm
(Eastern Time)
http://www.ada.gov

৯০ ৬

American Heart Association
1-800-242-8721
Hours: 24 hours a day, 7 days a week

৯০ ৬

American Lung Association
Lung Help Line 1-800-548-8252
to speak with a health care professional.
On the website, enter your zip code to find a chapter near you.
http://www.lungusa.org

৯০ ৬

Eldercare Locator
800-677-1116
Hours: Monday through Friday 9:00 am – 8:00 pm
(Eastern Time)
Locates services for seniors.
http://www.eldercare.gov

સ્જી   ન્જી

Mothers Against Drunk Drivers (MADD)
800-GET-MADD, (800-438-6233)
Hours: Monday through Friday 8:00 am – 5:00 pm
(Central Time)
http://www.madd.org

સ્જી   ન્જી

National Alzheimer's Association
1-800-272-3900
Hours: Monday through Friday, 8:00 am – 5:00 pm
(Eastern Time)
http://www.alz.org

સ્જી   ન્જી

National Cancer Institute
800-4-CANCER (800-422-6227)
http://www.nci.nih.gov

સ્જી   ન્જી

Depression and Bi-Polar Support Alliance
800-826-3632
Hours: Monday through Friday, 8:30 am – 5:30 pm
(Central Time)
http://www.dbsalliance.org

સ્જી   ન્જી

National Hospice and Palliative Care Organization
703-837-1500
Hours: Monday through Friday, 9:00 am – 6:00 pm
(Eastern Time)

http://www.nhpco.org

EATING DISORDERS

ॐ ॐ

**National Association of Anorexia Nervosa
and Associated Disorders**
1-847-831-3438
Monday through Friday, 9:00 am to 5 pm
(Central Time)
http://www.anad.org

ॐ ॐ

National Eating Disorders Association
603 Stewart Street, Suite 803
Seattle, WA 98101
1-800-931-2237
Hours: Monday through Friday, 8:30 am to 4:30 pm
(Pacific Time)
After hours, leave a message and someone will return your call
as soon as possible.

EMOTIONAL RESILIENCE

ॐ ॐ

CorStone
415-331-6161
CorStone (formerly, the International Center for Attitudinal
Healing) develops and supports emotional resilience in children,
families, and communities to better deal with

challenge, conflict, or crisis.
The organization provides comprehensive trainings and
facilitated peer support group services
around the world in the areas of:
aging, bereavement, HIV/AIDS, family resilience,
and children and youth conflict management programs.

CorStone's approach and philosophy is based on universal values
and the importance of embracing a positive attitude, love, and
forgiveness as the means towards making
peaceful and healthful choices.
http://www.corstone.org

GAY, LESBIAN, BISEXUAL, TRANSGENDER

ॐ ॐ

The Gay and Lesbian National Hotline
1-888-THE-GLNH (1-888-843-4564)
Hours: Volunteers attempt to be available for calls
Monday through Friday 4:00 pm to 12:00 am;
Saturday 12:00 noon to 5:00 pm (Eastern Time)
E-mail: glnh@glnh.org
A non-profit organization which provides nationwide toll-free
peer-counseling, information, and referrals.

ॐ ॐ

Parents and Friends of Lesbians and Gays (P-FLAG)
202-467-8180
Hours: Monday through Friday, 9:00 am – 5:30 pm

(Eastern Time)
550 local chapters for support, resources, and events.
http://www.pflag.org

ം ഏ

Pride Institute
1-800-547-7433
Hours: 24 hours a day, 7 days a week
Chemical dependency/mental health referral and information
hotline geared for the gay, lesbian, bisexual,
and transgender communities.
http://www.pride-institute.com

HIV/AIDS AND OTHER
SEXUALLY TRANSMITTED DISEASES

ം ഏ

AIDS INFO
1-800-HIV-0440 (1-800-448-0440)
TTY: 1-888-480-3739
International: 1-301-519-0459
Fax: 1-301-519-6616
Hours: Monday through Friday 12:00 pm to 5:00 pm
(Eastern Time)
Chat room: http://www.aidsinfo.nih.gov/livehelp,
12:00 pm to 4:00 pm, Monday through Friday
E-mail: contactus@aidsinfo.nih.gov
Callers can speak with experienced health specialists for
information about approved HIV treatment and help in locating
HIV/AIDS clinical trials across the USA.
In English, en Español.

ৰ্ক্ত ক্ষ

AIDS Treatment Data Network
1-800-734-7104 or 1-212-260-8868
Fax: 1-212-260-8869
Hours: Monday through Friday 9:00 am to 6:00 pm
(Eastern Time)

ৰ্ক্ত ক্ষ

CDC Business and Labor Resource Service
HIV/AIDS Workplace
1-877-242-9760
TTY: 1-800-243-7012
International: 1-301-562-1098
Fax: 1-888-282-7681
International Fax: 1-301-562-1050
Hours: Monday through Friday 9:00 am to 6:00 pm
(Eastern Time)
E-mail: info@hivatwork.org
In English, en Español.

ৰ্ক্ত ক্ষ

The Centers for Disease Control and Prevention (CDC)
National AIDS Clearinghouse
(Information and publication orders)
HIV/AIDS, Sexually Transmitted Diseases,
Viral Hepatitis, and Tuberculosis
1-800-458-5231
TTY: 1-800-243-1098
International: 1-404-679-3860
International TTY: 1-301-588-1586
Hours: Monday through Friday 9:00 am to 6:00 pm
(Eastern Time)

ক্ষ কত

CDC Information
1-800-CDC-INFO or 1-800-232-4636
TTY: 1-888-232-6348
Hours: 24 hours a day, 7 days a week
E-mail: cdcinfo@cdc.gov
In English, en Español.

ক্ষ কত

Elizabeth Glaser Pediatric AIDS Foundation
888-499-HOPE (4673)
http://www.pedaids.org

ক্ষ কত

Gay Men's Health Crisis
GMHC AIDS Hotline
1-800-AIDS-NYC (1-800-243-7692)
TTY: 1-212-645-7470
International: 1-212-807-6655
Hours: Monday through Friday 10:00 am to 9:00 pm
(Eastern Time)
Saturday, 12:00 to 3:00 pm
E-mail: hotline@gmhc.org
General AIDS hotline for those worried they may be infected,
or people wanting to access New York City AIDS resources.

ক্ষ কত

Hemophilia AIDS Network/
National Hemophilia Foundation
1-800-424-2634

International: 1-212-328-3700
Hours: Monday through Friday 9:00 am to 5:00 pm
(Eastern Time)

୬ ୬

National Association of People With AIDS Hotline
1-240-247-0880
Hours: Monday through Friday 9:00 am to 5:30 pm
(Eastern Time)

୬ ୬

National Herpes Hotline
1-919-361-8488
Hours: Monday through Friday 8:00 am to 5:00 pm
(Eastern Time)

୬ ୬

National Native American AIDS Prevention Center
1-720-382-2244
Fax: 1-720-382-2248
Hours: Monday through Friday 8:00 am to 5:00 pm
(Eastern Time)
E-mail: information@nnaapc.org

୬ ୬

National Prevention Information Network
1-800-458-5231 (English and Spanish)
TTY/TDD: 1-800-243-7012
International: 1-301-562-1098
Hours: Monday through Friday 9:00 am to 6:00 pm

(Eastern Time)
A national service for free educational materials about
HIV, TB, and other sexually transmitted diseases.

৵ ৵

National Sexually Transmitted Diseases (STD) Hotline
English: 1-800-227-8922
Spanish: 1-800-344-7432
7 days a week, 8:00 am to 2:00 am, Eastern Time
TTY/TDD: 1-800-243-7889
Hours: 24 hours a day, 7 days a week
Provides anonymous, confidential information on sexually
transmitted diseases (STDs) and how to prevent them.
Also, provides referrals to clinical and other services.

৵ ৵

Project Inform

National HIV/AIDS Treatment Infoline: 1-800-822-7422
or 1-866-HIV-INFO
International: 1-415-558-9051
Hours: Monday through Friday 10:00 am to 4:00 pm
(Pacific Time)

৵ ৵

TTY (Hearing Impaired) AIDS Hotline
800-243-7889

IANDS
The International Association for Near-Death Studies
Research, education, support, resources, conferences and more.
919-383-7940
http://www.iands.org

PETS

ॐ ॐ

Animal Chaplains
Animal chaplains and ministries providing:
Support, resources, multi-faith spiritual readings, animal
blessings, stories, blog,
become an animal chaplain, and much more.
http://www.animalchaplains.com

ॐ ॐ

American Society for the Prevention of Cruelty to Animals
1-212-876-7700
http://www.aspca.org

ॐ ॐ

Best Friends Animal Society
5001 Angel Canyon Road
Kanab, UT 84741
435-644-2001
On any given day there are about 2,000 cats, dogs, and other
animals that come from shelters and rescue groups
all across the country.

Best Friends is the largest
no kill animal sanctuary in the country.
For adoptions, education, volunteering, animal behavior
program, pet care tips, resource library, resources for rescuers,
health department, and much more.
http://www.bestfriends.org

SUICIDE

ॐ   ॐ

American Association of Suicidology
5221 Wisconsin Avenue, NW
Washington, DC 20015
Phone: (202) 237-2280
Fax: (202) 237-2282
Email: info@suicidology.org
Education and resources.
http://www.suicidology.org

ॐ   ॐ

The National Suicide Prevention Lifeline
1-800-273-TALK 1-800-273-8255
Access to trained telephone counselors,
24 hours a day, 7 days a week.

ॐ   ॐ

The Samaritans Suicide Prevention Hotline
1-212-673-3000
Hours: 24 hours a day, 7 days a week
Suicide crisis hotline.

৯০   ৩৬

Suicide Life Line Hotline
1-800-SUICIDE (1-800-784-2433)
Hours: 24 hours a day, 7 days a week

TEENS

৯০   ৩৬

Break the Cycle
888-988-8336
A non-profit organization engages, educates, and empowers
youths to build lives and communities free from
domestic and dating violence –
providing preventive education and outreach through
The Safe Place outboard.
http://www.breakthecycle.org

৯০   ৩৬

Boys and Girls Club
Type in your zip code for local chapters.
http://www.boysandgirlsclub.org

৯০   ৩৬

GLBT National Youth Talkline
1-800-246-7743
Hours: Monday – Friday 5:00 pm – 9:00 pm
(Pacific Time)
http://www.glbtnationalhealthbetter.org/talkline/index.html

༄ ༄

National Planned Parenthood
1-800-230-PLAN 1-800-230-7526
English and <u>Español</u>
Type in zip code to get local chapters in your area.
<u>http://www.NationalPlannedParenthood.org</u>

༄ ༄

National Runaway Switchboard
1-800-RUNAWAY (1-800-786-2929) Suicide 1-800-621-4000
TDD: 1-800-621-0394
Hours: 24 hours a day, 7 days a week
Crisis line for teenagers.

༄ ༄

Love is Respect National Teen Dating
1-866-331-9474
Chat on line and helpline.
Hours: 4 pm to midnight
(Central Time)
<u>http://www.loveisrespect.org</u>

༄ ༄

Teens Drug and Alcohol
Free Vibe
Teen approach to peer pressure, anti-drug message, and the
media. Personal stories, online games, and message boards.
Freevibe is the site for teens to get scientifically accurate drug
information, games, and tips for leading healthy lifestyles
and rejecting drugs.
<u>http://www.freevibe.com</u>

ଡ଼   ൶

Teen Wire
E-mail questions about relationships - all topics discussed.
http://www.TeenWire.com

ଡ଼   ൶

The Safe Place
The safe place, a project to break the cycle, is the most
comprehensive resource on the web where teens and young
adults can learn about domestic and dating violence,
as well as their legal rights and options.
http://www.thesafespace.org

ଡ଼   ൶

Women's Law
You must be at least 18 years old.
For legal information, type in the state where you live.
http://www.womenslaw.org

Sharon Lund

Front Body Diagram

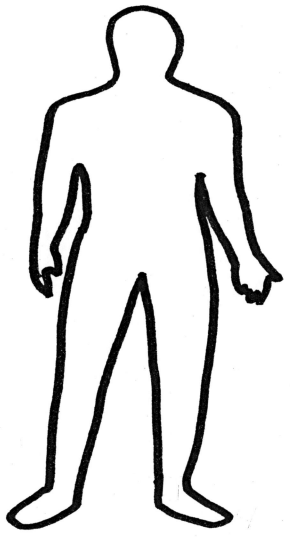

Front Body

Back Body Diagram

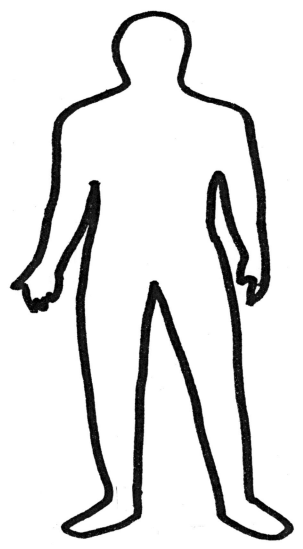

Back Body

ॐ   ॐ

Bibliography

Books:

Anodea, Judith PhD. *Wheels of Life: A User's Guide to the Chakra System*

Ashley-Farrand, Thomas. *Healing Mantras*

Balch, Phyllis A. *Prescriptions for Nutritional Healing*

Ban Breathnach, Sarah. *Simple Abundance*

Ban Breathnach, Sarah. *Simple Abundance Journal of Gratitude*

Beattie, Melody. *Beyond Codependency: And Getting Better All the Time*

Beattie, Melody. *Codependent No More: How to Stop Controlling Others and Start Caring for Yourself*

Blum, Ralph. *The Book of Runes*

Borysenko, Joan PhD. *Minding the Body, Mending the Mind*

Braden, Gregg. *Spontaneous Healing of Beliefs: Shattering the Paradigm of False Limits*

Branden, Nathaniel PhD. *How to Raise Your Self-Esteem: The Proven Action-Oriented Approach to Greater Self-Respect and Self-Confidence*

Branden, Nathaniel PhD. *Six Pillars of Self-Esteem*

Branden, Nathaniel PhD. *To See What I See and Know What I Know: A Guide to Self-Discovery*

Brennan, Barbara Ann. *Hands of Light: A Guide to Healing Through the Human Energy Field*

Browne, Sylvia. *Book of Angels*

Calborm, Cherie. *Juicing for Life: A Guide to Benefits of Fresh Fruit and Vegetable Juicing*

Calborm, Cherie, John. *Juicing, Fasting, and Detoxing for Life: Unleash the Healing Power of Fresh Juices and Cleansing Diets.*

Cameron, Julia and Bryan, Mark. *The Artist's Way: A Spiritual Path to Higher Consciousness*

Cameron, Julia. *Vein of Gold: A Journey to Your Creative Heart*

Cousins, Norman. *Anatomy of an Illness*

Daniel, Alma. Wyllie, Timothy. Ramer, Andre. *Ask Your Angels*

Demartini, John F. Dr. *Count Your Blessings: The Healing Power of Gratitude and Love*

Demartini, John. F. Dr. *The Heart of Love: How to Go Beyond Fantasy to Find True Relationship Fulfillment*

Dreher, Christine, CNN, CCH. *The Cleanse Cookbook*

Dyer, Wayne W. *Change Your Thoughts – Change Your Life: Living the Wisdom of the Tao*

Emoto, Masaru Dr. *The Hidden Messages in Water*

Fincher, Susanne F. *Coloring Mandalas 2: For Balance, Harmony, and Spiritual Well-Being*

Gawain, Shakti. *Creative Visualization: Use the Power of Your Imagination to Create What You Want In Your Life*

Goldberg, Burton *Alternative Medicine – The Definitive Guide*

Gregg, Susan. *The Encyclopedia of Angels, Spirit Guides and Ascended Masters: A Guide to 200 Celestial Beings to Help, Heal, and Assist You in Everyday Life*

Hansen, Taylor L. *He Walked the Americas*

Hay, Louise L. *The Power Is Within You*

Hay, Louise L. *You Can Heal Your Life*

Hicks, Esther and Jerry. *Ask and It is Given: Learning to Manifest Your Desires*

Hicks, Esther and Jerry. *The Amazing Power of Deliberate Intent*

Hicks, Esther and Jerry. *The Law of Attraction: The Basics of the Teachings of Abraham*

Holmes, Ernest. *The Science of Mind*

Jampolsky, Gerald G. MD. *A Mini Course for Life*

Katie, Byron. *Loving What Is: Four Questions That Can Change Your Life*

Khalsa, Singh Dharma MD. *The End of Karma*

Levine, Stephen and Ondrea. *A Year to Live – How to Live This Year as If It Were Your Last*

Levine, Stephen and Ondrea. *Unattended Sorrows: Recovering from Loss and Reviving the Heart*

Levine, Stephen and Ondrea. *Who Dies?: An Investigation of Conscious Living and Conscious Dying*

Lund, Sharon. *Sacred Living, Sacred Dying: A Guide to Embracing Life and Death*

Mark, Barbara. and Griswold, Trudy. *Angelspeake: How to Talk with Your Angels*

Millman, Dan. *Way of the Peaceful Warrior: A Book That Changes Lives*

Meyerowitz, Steve. *Juice Fasting and Detoxification: Use the Healing Power of Fresh Juice to Feel Young and Look Great*

Northrup, Christiane MD *Mother-Daughter Wisdom*

Northrup, Christiane MD *The Wisdom of Menopause*

Northrup, Christiane MD *Women's Bodies, Women's Wisdom*

Olson, Dale W. *The Pendulum Charts: Learn to Access Your Natural Intuitive Abilities and Take the Guesswork Out of Life*

Ponder, Catherine. *Open Your Mind to Receive*

Rumi. *The Illuminated Rumi*

Seeman Moreton, Valerie, N.D. *A New Day in Healing*

Seeman Moreton, Valerie, N.D. *Heal the Cause! Creating Wellness – Body, Mind & Spirit*

Simpson, Liz. *The Book of Chakra Healing*

Tipping, Colin. C. *Radical Forgiveness: Making Room for the Miracles*

Tolle, Eckhart. *The New Earth: Awakening to Your Life Purpose*
Walsch, Neale Donald. *Conversations with God: An Uncommon Dialogue*
Weiss, Brian. *Many Lives, Many Masters*
Young, Robert and Shelly. *The Ph Miracle for Weight Loss*

Other Resources

Cards Decks:

Virtue, Doreen PhD. *Goddess Guidance Oracle Cards*
Virtue, Doreen PhD. *Message from Your Angels*
Virtues Project, The. *Virtues Reflection Cards*
Young-Sowers, Meredith L. *Angelic Messenger CARDS: A Divination System for Spiritual Self-Discovery*

CDs:

Borysenko, Joan PhD. *Meditations for Relaxation and Stress Reduction*
Borysenko, Joan PhD. *Meditations for Self Healing and Inner Power*
Katie, Byron. *Your Inner Awakening: The Work of Byron Katie: Four Questions That Will Transform Your Life*
Klemp, Harold. *Hu: A Love Song*
Siegel, Bernie MD. *Meditations for Difficult Times*
Siegel, Bernie MD. *Meditations for Enhancing Your Immune System*
Siegel, Bernie MD. *Meditations for Finding the Key to Good Health*
Siegel, Bernie MD. *Meditations for Morning and Evening*
Siegel, Bernie MD. *Meditations for Peace of Mind*
Slap. Robert. *Eternal OM*

Weil, Andrew Dr. *Mindbody Toolkit: Experience Self Healing with Clinically Proven Techniques*

Movies and Videos:

Conscious Wave Director. *Walking Between the Worlds*
Darvich, Khashyar Director and Producer. *Dalai Lama Renaissance — Documentary*
Deutsch, Stephen Director. *Conversations with God*
Dunkerton, Martin Director and Producer. *Working Title: Think and Grow Rich*
Goorjian, Michael Director. *You Can Heal Your Life—The Movie*
Hagen, Monica Director. *Dying to Live: NDE—Documentary*
Heriot, Drew Director. *The Secret: Extended Edition 2006*
Perkul, Julia and Popova, Anastayia Directors. *Water – The Great Mystery*
Salva, Victor Director. *Peaceful Warrior*
Twyman, James F. Director. *The Moses Code —The Movie*
Vicente, Mark and Chasse, Betsy, Directors. *What the Bleep Do We Know!?*

Songs:

Florence, Jerry and Alliance. *I Love Myself The Way I Am*
Houston. Whitney. *A Hero Lies Within*

Miscellaneous:

Myss, Caroline and Occhiogrosso, Peter. *Sacred Contracts: The Journey — Game*
Rather, Dan. *TV Special — AIDS Hits Home*

Other References:

Abraham-Hicks. *Quote*
A Course in Miracles. *Quote*
Altschuler, Stuart. *Tell the Truth, Faster*
Blum, Ralph. *Vision Quest*
Buddha. *Quote*
Campbell, Joseph. *Quote.*
Christenson, Cassandra. *Project Nightlight*
Dorn, Ruth Eileen. *The Mask Project*
Dutton-Steindler, Linda. *Mentor*
Dyer, Wayne. Author *Quote*
Epictetus. *Quote*
Fisher, Sally. *AIDS Mastery Workshops*
Fisher, Sally. *Northern Lights Alternative*
Florence, Jerry and Alliance. *Song*
Forrest, Sharon Dr. *Vision Quest*
Forward, Susan, Ph.D. *Therapies*
Fox, Emmet. *Inner Child Description*
Halifax, Joan. *Vision Quest*
Hay, Louise L. *Hay Ride Support Group*
Holmes, Ernest. *Quote*
Houston, Whitney. *Song*
Jensen, Bernard Dr. *Quote*
Jung, Carl. *Archetypes Description and Quote*
Jung, Carl. *Inner Child Description*
Kostka, Claus. *Family Constellation Workshops*
Kubler-Ross, Elisabeth, MD. *Workshop and Quote*
Lazaris, Jach Pursel. *Workshops*
Levine, Stephen and Ondrea. *Workshops*
McGraw, Phil, Dr. *Quote*
Nanh, Thich Nhat. *Retreat*
Orr, Leonard. *Quote*
Robbins, Anthony. *Four Day Workshop*

Swaine, Clinton. ***Frontier Trainings: The World Leader in Experiential Games Technology***

Weil, Andrew Dr. ***Quote***

Whitefield, Charles. ***Inner Child Description***

Williamson, Marianne. ***Los Angeles Center for Living***

Notes

_____

_____

_____

_____

_____

_____

_____

_____

_____

_____

_____

_____

_____

_____

_____

_____

_____

_____

_____

Printed in the United States
140315LV00001B/4/P